JUDICIAL ROULETTE

JUDICIAL ROULETTE

Report of the Twentieth Century Fund
Task Force on Judicial Selection

Background Paper by David M. O'Brien

 Priority Press Publications/New York/1988

The Twentieth Century Fund is a research foundation undertaking timely analyses of economic, political, and social issues. Not-for-profit and non-partisan, the Fund was founded in 1919 and endowed by Edward A. Filene.

Library of Congress Cataloging-in-Publication Data
O'Brien, David M.
  Judicial roulette
  "A Twentieth Century Fund task force report"
  Bibliography: p.
  Includes index.
  1. Judges—United States—Selection and appointment.
I. O'Brien, David M. II. Twentieth Century Fund.
Task Force on Judicial Selection.
KF8776.J85   1988 347.73'14   88-9773
                347.30714

ISBN: 0-87078-226-6
ISBN: 0-87078-225-8 (pbk.)

Foreword

A LITTLE OVER TWO YEARS AGO, the staff and Trustees of the Twentieth Century Fund decided that the way in which the federal judiciary was selected needed review. After some deliberation, it was decided that the issue was so timely and controversial that it warranted discussion and evaluation by a Task Force. A group of experts who could knowledgeably examine a system of judicial selection that seemed to be growing ever more political was thus brought together to explore the ways in which candidates for the federal bench—both the lower federal courts and the Supreme Court—are selected, nominated, and confirmed.

No one realized at the time just how confrontational the process would become. The public furor that erupted over President Reagan's nomination of Judge Bork, and then of Judge Ginsburg, brought the judicial selection system into public view and made clear that the nominating process is of very real concern to the American people.

The members of the Task Force watched these events with great interest, examining them in the context of past Supreme Court nominations and determining how they related to the overall problem of judicial selection. While basically agreeing that the current system works, the Task Force decided that there were specific changes that would make the process more efficient—and more likely to result in the selection of better judges.

The Fund is grateful to David O'Brien for his thoughtful and comprehensive background paper. It also is grateful to the members of the Task Force—and particularly to its chairman, Hugh Carey—for persevering through numerous and difficult meetings. The Task Force debated long and hard over this Report, often disagreeing sharply on what to recommend—which is reflected in their dissents—but finally arrived at the judiciously wrought recommendations presented therein.

M. J. Rossant, DIRECTOR
The Twentieth Century Fund
March 1988

Contents

Members of the Task Force

Hugh L. Carey, *chairman*
Former Governor of New York State; Executive Vice President, W. R. Grace & Co., New York

Walter Berns
John M. Olin University Professor, Georgetown University; Resident Scholar, American Enterprise Institute for Public Policy Research, Washington, D.C.

Joseph A. Califano, Jr.
Partner, Dewey, Ballantine, Bushby, Palmer & Wood, Washington, D.C.

Lloyd N. Cutler
Partner, Wilmer, Cutler & Pickering, Washington, D.C.

Philip B. Kurland
William R. Kenan, Jr., Distinguished Service Professor, University of Chicago Law School

Jack W. Peltason
Chancellor, University of California, Irvine

Nicholas J. Spaeth
Attorney General, North Dakota

Michael M. Uhlmann
Partner, Pepper, Hamilton & Scheetz, Washington, D.C.

Robert F. Wagner
Former Mayor of New York City; Adviser, Home Group, New York

David M. O'Brien, *rapporteur*
Associate Professor, Woodrow Wilson Department of Government and Foreign Affairs, University of Virginia

REPORT OF THE
TASK FORCE

I N THE FEDERALIST PAPERS, Number 78, Alexander Hamilton wrote that "the complete independence of the Courts of justice is peculiarly essential" in a Republic governed by a "limited Constitution." "The courts must declare the sense of the law," Hamilton continued, "and if they should be disposed to exercise WILL instead of JUDGMENT, the consequence would be the substitution of their pleasure for that of the legislative body."

The principle of judicial independence requires that members of the federal bench be further removed from the people and the pressures of public opinion than are other public officials. Appointed by the president with the advice and consent of the Senate (not the House, the more popular branch of the legislature), the judges of both the supreme and the lower federal courts were to serve for life—removable only upon conviction for an impeachable offense—and were assured a compensation that was not to be diminished "during their Continuance in Office." They were to be free of political control because it was understood that the power they were to exercise was not political.

Today's federal judiciary exercises more power over a broader range of social and economic issues than the framers of the Constitution ever envisaged. Federal courts now play an active role in shaping and carrying out social policy, passing on the legality of governmental decisions as to a wide range of issues from school desegregation to affirmative action and abortion.

Informed opinion differs widely about the virtues and liabilities of the current role of the federal courts, but most observers agree that the courts' role is unlikely to be diminished in the near future. Most observers also agree that the expanded public policy role of the federal courts has intensified the problems inherent in the politics of selecting judges. Urging or blocking particular judicial appointments is increasingly regarded as a way to further policy goals. Thus, candidates for the federal bench are now subjected to intense scrutiny not only of their knowledge and understanding of the law but also of their positions on policy issues.

Unfortunately, choosing candidates for anything other than their legal qualifications damages the public's perception of the institutional prestige of the judiciary and calls into question the high ideal of judicial independence.

Nevertheless, this Task Force—composed of former public officials, professors of law, politicians, journalists, and political scientists—believes that, on the whole, the traditional process of appointing federal judges by the executive with the advice and consent of the Senate has worked reasonably well. Certainly, we do not think that major changes are called for. We do believe that several recent developments threaten the efficiency, stature, and independence of the federal judiciary. We are therefore making recommendations for reforms, some of which may prove controversial, to enhance the prospects of attracting highly qualified judges and to promote the tradition of judicial independence that Hamilton prized so highly.

Historically, presidents have tended to nominate and the Senate to confirm those who have demonstrated loyalty to the president's party or at least a general sympathy with the president's policy goals. On balance, this tradition has proven salutary. Broadly speaking, it is the means by which the courts are aligned or realigned with the rest of the nation. Yet there has been an increasing tendency for recent administrations, Democratic as well as Republican, to use the judicial appointment process to serve more specific political objectives. President Jimmy Carter openly exercised "affirmative action" in judicial selection to create a more "representative" and "balanced" federal judiciary. Many people have charged that President Ronald Reagan's nominees for federal judgeships have depended more on his perception of their support for his social agenda than on their competence and standing in the legal community.

Maintaining Standards

This Task Force recognizes that judicial appointments cannot be made free of political considerations. It is our view that eliminating political considerations would not be desirable. Thus, it is inevitable that, on occasion, meritorious individuals may not be nominated or, if nominated, may be denied confirmation for political reasons, no matter which political party holds the White House or which controls the Senate.

At the same time, *the Task Force believes that a demonstration of the requisite qualifications for judicial competence—including temperament, professional training, experience, and personal integrity—is the indispen-*

sable sine qua non for nomination by a president and confirmation by the Senate. As Justice Felix Frankfurter once so eloquently put it, "the most relevant things about an appointee are his breadth of vision, his imagination, his capacity for disinterested judgment, his power to discover and to suppress his prejudices."[1]

Attaining greater precision in setting standards for judging the attributes and qualifications of judicial nominees has long been considered desirable. But precise and bipartisan standards for selecting a "meet person, learned in the law," have proved—and are likely to continue to prove—elusive, if only because such qualities as "judicial temperament" and "dispassionate judgment" are difficult to define. Even objective standards, such as the American Bar Association's criteria for age and years of legal experience, may on occasion be appropriately outweighed by other qualifications.

Accordingly, the members of the Task Force believe that any set of objective standards must be flexible, varying with each level of the federal judicial system because of the different functions of the district (trial) courts, appellate courts, and the Supreme Court. Certain qualities, such as demonstrated disinterestedness and knowledge of the law, are essential for all federal judges; but because different skills are required at different levels of the judiciary, different considerations ought to come into play in the selection and confirmation of federal judges at each level. The difficulty of establishing reasonably objective criteria for the appointment of judges is not a reason to abandon the effort, or an excuse to convert the nomination and confirmation process into a struggle for political advantage.

Thus, for district court judgeships, greater attention should be paid to nominating those with extensive trial experience. Because they sit alone when adjudicating cases or overseeing juries, district judges need certain technical skills and experience in the courtroom. These skills are not as important for those appointed to the appellate bench, where cases are decided in collegial fashion and where other skills, such as demonstrated ability to write and think clearly and to take a broader perspective in analyzing legal problems, should be given greater weight.

At the Supreme Court level, emphasis should be placed on attracting candidates who have displayed an extraordinary capacity for jurisprudential thought and statesmanship. As Learned Hand put it in his 1930 address "Sources of Tolerance":

it is as important to a judge called upon to pass on a question of constitutional law, to have at least a bowing acquaintance with Acton and Maitland, with Thucydides, Gibbon and Carlyle, with Homer, Dante, Shakespeare and Milton, with Machiavelli, Montaigne and Rabelais, with Plato, Bacon, Hume and Kant, as with the books which have been specifically written on the subject.[2]

Unless judges possess the indispensable qualifications set forth above, they should not be nominated or confirmed. Judges should not be selected merely because they are believed to adhere to some preferred judicial philosophy.

The Task Force acknowledges that "representative" considerations have and will at various times come properly into play in judicial appointments. Geographical representation on the Supreme Court was important in establishing the legitimacy of the Court and the national government in the nineteenth century, an era when sectional loyalty was far greater than it is now. Today, as our population has become increasingly diverse and opportunities have widened, it has become equally important that the federal bench be broadly reflective of that diversity. But the concept of "representation," while not illegitimate for presidential and senatorial consideration, is not in itself a sufficient qualification for those nominated to serve on the federal bench. Nominees should not be chosen or confirmed solely on the basis of race or sex, religion or ethnic background any more than on the basis of ideology. At the same time, the Task Force recommends that strong efforts be made to ensure that all qualified candidates are considered fairly, particularly those from groups that historically have been discriminated against.

In addition, the members of the Task Force believe that judicial recruitment, especially in the lower courts, has been and will continue to be seriously hampered because judicial salaries have not kept pace with the salaries of leading lawyers in private practice. As many studies and commissions have recommended, *the Task Force urges Congress and the administration to consider not only increasing the salaries of federal judges but providing improved life insurance coverage and annuity benefits. Furthermore, the Task Force recommends that judicial salaries no longer be tied to congressional salaries and that a supplementary allowance be provided for judges sitting in areas where the cost of living is recognized to be appreciably higher than elsewhere in the country.**

---

* *Lloyd N. Cutler dissents:* While strongly supporting substantial increases in judicial salaries, I do not agree with this recommendation. *Philip B. Kurland also dissents* from the recommendation that there be a provision for a supplementary allowance.

Changing the Process

Because of the importance of securing high-quality judicial appointments, *the Task Force proposes certain procedural changes in the confirmation process.* Our changes would not require a constitutional amendment. Quite simply, they are geared to focus more attention on judicial training and the experience and reputation of nominees. That is the primary basis on which nominees should be judged. The only feasible way of enhancing the prospects for judgments on this basis and improving the quality of the federal bench is by bringing more light to bear on the legal qualifications of judicial nominees.

In recommending changes in the confirmation process, the Task Force recognizes that presidents have the constitutional right to set their own criteria for selecting nominees, even when their choices run against professional or public opinion. In the future, we will continue to expect presidents to appoint those who share their own visions of legal and social policy. We acknowledge that the standards employed by the Senate when confirming judicial nominees are also likely to reflect the same mix of political and policy considerations as any other legislative vote. But both the president and the Senate should have the same goal in mind when judging candidates for the bench—choosing the well-qualified candidates to serve.

The primary problem with the confirmation process for district and appellate court judges is that the Senate too often gives "rubber stamp" approval to nominees. The Senate Judiciary Committee's confirmation hearings on lower-court judges are usually superficial, lasting five minutes or less, and the Senate's vote to confirm nominees is more often than not a mere formality. In short, the problem with the confirmation process for lower-court judges is a lack of accountability because the process lacks visibility.

Therefore, *the Task Force favors the practice adopted by some senators and states of employing bipartisan nominating commissions that screen and recommend possible nominees for openings in the state and lower federal courts.* To the extent that judicial nominating commissions are politically balanced and include leaders in state and local bar associations, they also may contribute to recruiting high-caliber judges for the federal bench.

At a minimum, confirmation hearings on nominees for the lower courts should be announced in advance with notices in appropriate legal newspapers and the periodicals of state and local bar associations. In addition, the Task Force is in general agreement that the Senate's ad-

vice and consent function under the Constitution could be made more effective were a subcommittee to conduct open hearings in the locale in which a nominee would be seated on the federal bench.

Notices of nominations and hearings should be published and invitations to appear issued to all relevant state and local bar associations. If a nominee's sponsoring senator or a representative of the Department of Justice wishes to offer testimony, he should be heard as well. The subcommittee would then report its findings and recommendations to the full committee.

Such a change would go a long way toward having the Senate give serious rather than cursory consideration to the qualifications and backgrounds of judicial nominees. Although this change could expose the appointment process to greater pressure from special-interest-group politics, it would give the process greater visibility and accountability. It would also reduce the risk of "cronyism," thereby enhancing public respect for those serving on the federal bench.

The Task Force believes that the fundamental problem with the confirmation process for Supreme Court nominees is just the opposite of that for lower-court nominees: it is too visible and attracts too much publicity.* In some cases, such as the nominations of Louis Brandeis,

---

* *Joseph A. Califano, Jr., dissents:* I disagree with the conclusions of the Task Force Report that the confirmation process for Supreme Court nominees is too visible and attracts too much publicity. I also disagree with the conclusion that Supreme Court nominees should no longer be expected to appear as witnesses during the Senate Judiciary Committee hearings on confirmation. Accordingly, I dissent from most of the discussion and other conclusions in the Task Force discussion of the confirmation process for Supreme Court nominees.

Much of the Supreme Court portion of the Task Force report is a thinly tailored argument to repeal the First Amendment to the Constitution as it might apply to hearings on Supreme Court nominees. The public scrutiny of Supreme Court nominees during their testimony before the Senate Judiciary Committee and such scrutiny of the testimony of other witnesses before the committee are essential in our society.

Each of the 9 members of the Supreme Court has far more power than any one of the 100 senators and certainly any one of the 435 representatives. Each Supreme Court nominee should be subjected to widespread public scrutiny before confirmation. This is of the essence in a free society in which one of the branches exercises an enormous amount of power—indeed, final power in some matters—with respect to the other two branches and to the people of the country.

John Parker, Felix Frankfurter, Justice Abe Fortas to be chief justice, and Robert Bork, the confirmation process has come dangerously close to looking like the electoral process. It has become very much a national referendum on the appointment, with media campaigns, polling techniques, and political rhetoric that distract attention from, and sometimes completely distort, the legal qualifications of the nominee.*

Since the appointment of Justice Sandra Day O'Connor in 1981, confirmation hearings on Supreme Court nominees have been televised. Media coverage may have a salutary effect in informing and educating the public about the nominee, the Court, and the Constitution. But it has also invited abuse of the confirmation process. The White House, the Department of Justice, senators, witnesses, and even nominees now seem tempted to use televised hearings as a forum for other purposes, ranging from self-promotion to mobilizing special interest groups in order to influence public opinion. Witnesses are called to testify not principally for their legal expertise, but as advocates for and against the nominees and as representatives of competing interests and constituencies. The confirmation process, in short, has become extremely politicized in a way that denigrates the Court and serves to undermine its prestige as well as public respect for the rule of law.

The Task Force recognizes that nominations to the Supreme Court have long had, and will continue to have, high visibility. The clock on media coverage, especially television coverage, cannot and should not be turned back. But in light of that extensive media coverage, *the confirmation process needs to be depoliticized by minimizing the potential*

As Congress legislates in more detail, it puts more and more issues into our federal judiciary. As science raises to the level of constitutional dispute a host of issues that involve life and death—abortion is the most explosive one today, but surely euthanasia lurks in the wings—it puts more and more issues before our federal judiciary. As a citizen, I want to know as much as possible about each of the nine people who are going to decide such issues for me and my country.

Therefore, I believe that Senate confirmation hearings and the entire selection process for Supreme Court Justices should be as public and as publicized as modern communications can make them.

* *Philip B. Kurland strongly dissents* both from the conclusion of this paragraph and from the implication that these five hearings are analogous in any relevant way.

for participants to posture and distort the basic purpose of the proceedings.*

Except in cases where a candidate's personal conduct—what the Constitution terms the "good behavior" requisite for all federal judges—is at issue, the Task Force recommends that Supreme Court nominees *should no longer be expected to appear as witnesses during the Senate Judiciary Committee's hearings on their confirmation.*** (If they ask to do so, they should, of course, be permitted to appear.)

This recommendation calls for the Senate once again to adhere to the practice that it followed for most of its history. Throughout the past century, Supreme Court nominees did not appear as witnesses. It was not until 1925, when Harlan F. Stone made an appearance before the Judiciary Committee, that a Supreme Court nominee did so. In 1939, Felix Frankfurter was the second Supreme Court nominee to appear and to answer senators' questions, though he pointed out that it was "not only bad taste but inconsistent with the duties of the office for which I have been nominated for me to attempt to supplant my past record by personal declaration." A decade later, Sherman Minton repeatedly refused to appear before the committee, explaining that his "record speaks for itself."[3]

The practice of Supreme Court nominees appearing and answering questions before the Senate Judiciary Committee is a relatively recent one. It is one that now ought to be abandoned. But *if nominees continue to appear before the committee, then the Task Force recommends that senators should not put questions to nominees that call for answers that would indicate how they would deal with specific issues if they were confirmed.* This was the practice until quite recently. During the confirmation hearings on Justice O'Connor and Judge Bork, the questions and answers sometimes crossed this line.[4] Unfortunately, this change contributes further to the politicization of the process. In the Task Force's view, when nominees give answers indicating how they will vote once confirmed, they destroy the public's belief in the fairness of those on the bench, and thereby undermine confidence in the Court.

---

* *Walter Berns comments:* I suggest further that television cameras be banned from the hearings. This would go some way toward getting the senators to attend to the business at hand instead of striking poses to please their favorite constituents.

** *Lloyd N. Cutler dissents.*

*The Task Force further recommends that the Judiciary Committee and the Senate base confirmation decisions on a nominee's written record and the testimony of legal experts as to his competence.** The hearings, the witnesses called to testify, and the questions asked of them should be confined to the ability and capacity of the nominee to carry out the high tasks of serving on the Supreme Court.

The members of the Task Force are aware that these recommendations are controversial. The politics of judicial selection are such that any attempt to interfere with the procedures that have evolved also will interfere with the prerogatives of well-established political interests. Moreover, there was and continues to be considerable debate, and differences of opinion, among members of the Task Force on several important issues. But it is the view of the Task Force that the recommendations made in this report can contribute to restoring the basic purpose of confirmation hearings: to ensure that we select competent, impartial, and thoughtful judges. In addition, the Task Force believes that its recommendations, if adopted, could do much to rebuild public confidence in the appointment process, the Supreme Court, and the federal judiciary. We speak with one voice in acknowledging the importance of the issues raised in this examination of the politics of judicial selection and in affirming, with Hamilton, that "the complete independence of the courts of justice" is an indispensable prerequisite for the judiciary in a democratic polity.

---

* *Lloyd N. Cutler dissents.*

Notes

1. Philip B. Kurland, ed., *Felix Frankfurter on the Supreme Court: Extrajudicial Essays on the Court and the Constitution* (Cambridge, Mass.: Harvard University Press, 1970), p. 216.

2. Learned Hand, *The Spirit of Liberty,* ed. Irving Dillard (New York: Vintage Books, 1959), p. 63.

3. Quotations from Ronald Collins and David M. O'Brien, "Just Where Does Judge Bork Stand?" *The National Law Journal,* September 7, 1987, pp. 13, 29.

4. For the argument that Supreme Court nominees should discuss their views and how they may vote on specific issues, see Grover Rees III, "Questions for Supreme Court Nominees at Confirmation Hearings: Excluding the Constitution," *Georgia Law Review* 17 (1983), p. 913. (During President Reagan's second term, Rees was an assistant attorney general in the Department of Justice, with responsibilities for screening judicial nominees. He is now a judge for the territorial court for Samoa.) For an argument against nominees promising how they will vote, once confirmed, on particular cases, see David M. O'Brien and Ronald Collins, "Bork's Shifts Made Credibility An Issue," *The Baltimore Sun,* October 11, 1987, pp. K1, K3.

BACKGROUND PAPER

by David M. O'Brien

· 1 ·

The Federal Bench
and Public Policy

D EBATE over judicial appointments is complex and runs back to what the Founding Fathers sought to achieve in the Constitution. By giving the president the power to nominate and—with the advice and consent of the Senate—appoint federal judges, the Constitution provided a prescription for political struggle as much as an invitation for cooperation and compromise.

The greater role of the courts in the development of legal and social policy makes judicial selection even more critical. Debate is likely to continue as significant questions remain unanswered. Are judgeships, like other political appointments, simply a matter of presidential patronage—a presidential prerogative? How far may presidents go in pursuing their legal-policy goals through judicial appointments? What is the Senate's role in offering "advice and consent"? On what basis does—or should—the Senate confirm or reject nominees? Has judicial selection become too politicized? Does the Senate acquiesce too much on Supreme Court nominees in an effort to preserve its own patronage over lower federal court judges? Is there a better way to appoint judges?

There are other aspects to the debate. Some argue that the federal bench, which historically has been a bastion of white Anglo-Saxon Protestant males, should be more representative in terms of race, religion, gender, and ethnicity—particularly since it has grown so enormously over the past thirty years. The Carter administration made a concerted effort to appoint women, blacks, Hispanics, and Asians. By comparison, very few of these have been named by the Reagan administration; claims have been made about the difficulty of finding well-qualified minorities, and there are those—like Justice Harlan F. Stone—who do not believe "that in addition to political considerations, considerations of race, re-

15

ligion and sectional interests should influence the appointment" of judges.[1] What weight should such concerns be given in the selection and confirmation process?

These questions turn back on the central issues: What standards should apply in the selection and confirmation—or rejection—of nominees? Should judges be held to a higher standard than other political appointees? If not, then what (if anything) is wrong with the president making partisan appointments or the Senate rejecting those nominees solely on partisan grounds? What is the possibility of achieving agreement, as professors Laurence Tribe and Philip Kurland recently urged, on a nonpartisan standard for judicial appointments—one that would guarantee appointments of high caliber while flexible enough to preserve presidential and senatorial interests?[2] If such standards are possible, how might they be established and applied? What institutional arrangements could be used to implement them?

"A Government of Laws, Not of Men"

The ideal of a "government of laws, not of men" is grounded in the constitutional provision that federal judges hold lifetime tenure, subject only to removal by impeachment, not by the ebb and flow of political-party power. It is fortified by a tradition of judicial independence and by popular expectations of impartial justice.[3]

Federal judges, who are appointed largely for political reasons, must demonstrate that they are not "the president's men," regardless of why or how they got on the bench.[4] As Justice Felix Frankfurter put it, they should be "legal monks."[5] They are expected to remove themselves from politics, when necessary rule in ways that may disappoint their presidential benefactors, and even challenge—or thwart—popular will. To the extent that the judicial appointment process is (or is perceived to be) determined by partisanship, the legitimacy of the courts and the ideal of "a government of laws, not of men" are threatened.

Though federal judges are not directly accountable to those who appoint them—except by impeachment, which Thomas Jefferson called a "mere scarecrow"[6]—courts are broadly responsive to the public will. This is so because the appointment process is a political process that permits the infusion of democratic values into the judiciary and serves as a curb on the courts. With shifts in electoral politics, the selection and composition of those serving on the federal bench change, and the courts and country are aligned or headed for confrontation.

The appointment of judges thus involves a delicate balance on which hangs the myth and reality of "a government of laws, not of men." At the fulcrum, the politics of judicial appointments gives life to "the rule of law."

The Increasing Size and Role of the Federal Judiciary

Over the past thirty years, the caseload in the lower federal courts—the district and appellate courts—has risen sharply. And with the growth in caseloads, the number of judges has increased dramatically. For example, while the number of district court judges doubled between 1900 and 1960, over the past twenty years it has more than doubled again.[7] In 1986, there were 576 district court judges (and another 156 on senior status, taking cases as workloads demanded).[8] Figure 1.1 shows the growth in the number of district and appellate court judges since 1930.

Along with the increase in the number of judges, there has been a significant growth in support staff, and thus in the size of the entire judiciary. Between 1970 and 1980, judicial personnel swelled by 111 percent; it now numbers almost 15,000.[9] In 1986, more than 1,700 law clerks, over 1,000 secretaries, 130 staff attorneys, 60 district and circuit court executives and staff, and some 50 clerks and related employees supported the 836 district and circuit court judges (of which 197 were retired). Remaining judiciary personnel include probation staff, bankruptcy judges, magistrates, and public defenders.

These trends have led some judges and commentators to warn of the "bureaucratization of the judiciary,"[10] and they underscore the importance of high-quality appointments. But, according to Justice Antonin Scalia in a recent speech to the American Bar Association, if caseloads and workloads are not reduced, finding "the best and the brightest" for the bench may become impossible.[11]

One problem is that judges' salaries are not high enough to lure legal talent away from more lucrative law practices. Chief Justice William H. Rehnquist, like his predecessor, has pressed for pay increases in order to draw "first-rate talent" into the judiciary. As a result, in 1987, the salaries of district court judges rose by 10 percent, the salaries of those on the appellate bench by 11 percent, and the salaries of the justices by less than 3 percent. District court judges now make $81,100 a year, appellate judges earn $85,700, and associate justices of the Supreme Court draw salaries of $107,200. The chief justice makes $111,700, due to his additional administrative duties. But these figures still pale in comparison

Figure 1.1

Number of Lower-Court Judges
1930-86

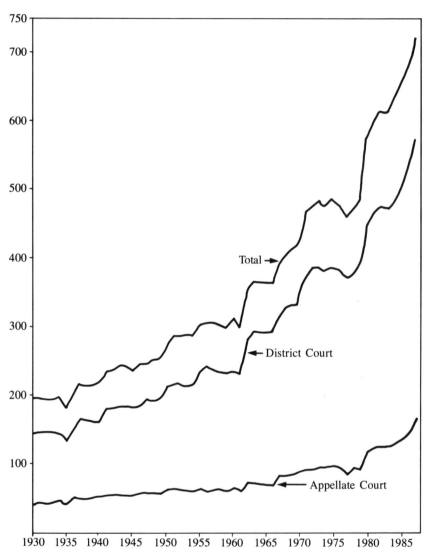

to salaries of the top partners in leading law firms, which range well above $250,000 a year.[12]

Another, more serious, problem stems from the increasing flow of litigation—that is, the decline in appellate review. District courts have largely become courts of first and last resort. In 1985, for example, less than 10 percent of all civil cases—and only a slightly higher percentage of criminal cases—were appealed. As one judge concluded, "justice stops in the district."[13]

The decline in appellate review is even greater in the appellate courts. Ten years ago, Ninth Circuit Judge Shirley Hufstedler noted that "the Supreme Court now hears fewer than one percent of the cases decided by the federal courts of appeal."[14] In 1986, former Harvard Law School Dean Erwin Griswold stated that "less than half of one percent, that is, less than one case out of every two hundred decided by the court of appeals is actually reviewed by the Supreme Court."[15] The growing number of circuit court judges and the growing size of the circuit courts contribute to the decline in national appellate review and to a breakdown of cohesiveness, uniformity, and certainty in national law and legal policy.[16]

No less significant is the changing nature of business coming to federal courts. The courts are now deciding questions of social policy that would have been virtually unthinkable fifty, twenty, or even ten years ago. The most divisive issues—abortion, homosexual rights, reverse discrimination, government liability, and others on the frontiers of science and technology—that courts must decide fuel debate over judicial policymaking. In addition, shifts in the routine work of the courts continue to take place. The business of district courts, for example, is evolving toward less criminal and more civil litigation. The critical point is that the role of federal courts in fashioning national law and policy has grown enormously. As Justice Lewis F. Powell, Jr., put it, "the judiciary may be the most important instrument for social, economic and political change."[17]

The increase in caseloads, changes in the business coming before the federal courts, and the growth both of the federal bench and of the role of the courts in implementing national public policy make judicial appointments a critical policy tool—especially for presidents who want to influence the direction of the judiciary and the course of public law and policy long after they have left office.

Judgeships as Symbols of Presidential Power

Historically, except when a seat opened up on the Supreme Court, judgeships usually did not spark political controversy. And while Supreme Court vacancies have long been invested with a great deal of political symbolism, they occur only infrequently—at the rate of about one every two years. Four presidents had no opportunity to name Supreme Court justices. Lower-court judgeships have only recently acquired greater political visibility. This is, in part, because of their growing number; it is also because recent presidents have sought to make them symbols of their own power.

Judgeships tend to take on greater political symbolism when the norms of the appointment process are challenged or transformed. It was thus in 1937 when the Senate battled President Franklin D. Roosevelt over his "Court-packing" plan. Virtually all of the early New Deal legislation had been thwarted by a conservative majority on the Court. Emboldened by his landslide reelection in 1936, FDR struck back. His plan was to increase the number of justices from nine to fifteen; he thereby hoped to secure a majority favorable to his social and economic programs. Bipartisan forces in the Senate and public opinion, however, defeated his attempt to make the Court a symbol of his own power. Although his "Court-packing" plan failed, FDR succeeded in infusing his political philosophy into the Court by filling nine vacancies during his remaining years in office.

Not until Richard M. Nixon's 1968 presidential campaign did judgeships again take on such great political symbolism. Nixon's election set the stage for a transformation in the politics of judicial appointments, for high on Nixon's agenda was returning "law and order" to the country through the appointment of "strict constructionists" and judicial conservatives.

After Nixon, federal judgeships became a more potent political symbol. Jimmy Carter sought to make the bench more representative by naming women, blacks, Hispanics, and other ethnic minorities. Ronald Reagan promised to appoint only those supportive of "traditional family values" and opposed to abortion and past judicial activism.[18]

The higher visibility now given to federal judgeships illustrates how the politics of the appointment process has changed. In July and August 1986, public attention was captured by the confirmation hearings on Reagan's nomination of Justice William Rehnquist as successor to retiring Chief Justice Warren E. Burger and of Judge Antonin Scalia to fill the seat vacated by Rehnquist. It was only the second time in history that such hearings were televised; the first televised confirmation hearings were those of Reagan's initial appointee to the Court, Justice Sandra Day O'Connor. The vast majority of hearings on lower-court judges last less than five minutes, with only a presiding senator and the nominee present. By comparison, over 60 percent of the public followed Rehnquist's hearings.[19]

Subsequently, during a week-long countrywide stumping effort in late October before the 1986 congressional elections, Reagan unsuccessfully urged voters to reelect Republicans to ensure Senate confirmation of his judicial nominees. For the first time, federal judgeships became a major issue in Senate races. In at least one state—Washington—it turned out to be the central issue. During the battle over the controversial nomination of Daniel Manion to the Court of Appeals for the Seventh Circuit, Republican Senator Slade Gorton traded his vote in order to win the Department of Justice's endorsement of his choice (William Dwyer) for a district court judgeship in his home state of Washington. That well-publicized instance of vote-trading—in the face of widespread criticism of Manion by the legal profession and a sitting federal judge on the Seventh Circuit Court of Appeals—allowed for Manion's confirmation by a sharply divided vote of 48 to 46, but gave Gorton's Democratic opponent a campaign issue that cost Gorton reelection. In that and other races, the Democratic Senatorial Campaign Committee and the Fund for a Democratic Majority successfully made judgeships an issue in fund-raising.

Judgeships as Instruments of Presidential Power

Judgeships have become not merely a symbol but an instrument of power and a way to ensure a president's legacy. As the size of the judiciary has grown, there have been many more judgeships to hand out, and, in turn, their political significance has grown. From 1981 through mid-1987, Reagan appointed over three hundred judges. There is a possibility that he will name over half of all lower-court judges in the country before he leaves the Oval Office. No other president has named as many. Through these judicial appointments, Attorney General Edwin Meese has said, the administration may "institutionalize the Reagan revolution so it can't be set aside no matter what happens in future presidential

Table 1.1

Number of Judges Named by Presidents from FDR to Reagan

	FDR	Truman	Eisenhower	Kennedy	Johnson	Nixon	Ford	Carter	Reagan[a]
Supreme Court	9	4	5	2	2	4	1	0	4
Circuit Court	52	27	45	20	41	45	12	56	76
District Court	137	102	127	102	125	182	52	206	258
Special Courts[b]	14	9	10	2	13	7	1	3	6
Totals:	212	142	187	126	181	238	66	265	344

[a]The number of Reagan appointees includes those through 1987. As of January 1, 1988, there were an additional fifty-eight nominees or vacancies remaining to be acted on and another thirty to forty expected before the expiration of Reagan's term.
[b]Includes Customs, Customs and Patent Appeals, and Court of International Trade.

Table 1.2

Sitting Judges on the Courts of Appeals in 1986 According to Presidential Appointments*

Circuit	FDR	Truman	Eisenhower	Kennedy	Johnson	Nixon	Ford	Carter	Reagan
First			(1)		1	1		2	2
Second		(1)	(1)	1	1	1 (2)	1	2	6
Third	(1)		(1)		2	5 (2)		2	3
Fourth			(1)		1 (1)	2 (1)	1	4	3 (1)
Fifth			(2)		(2)	2 (1)		6 (1)	6
Sixth			(2)	(1)	(2)	2		5 (1)	9 (1)
Seventh			(1)	(1)	1 (1)	(1)		1	7
Eighth					2 (1)	1	(1)	2	4
Ninth			(4)	1 (1)	1	3 (2)	2	13	5
Tenth			(1)	(3)		1 (1)		3	3
Eleventh			(1)		1 (2)			5 (1)	1
Federal		(1)	1 (1)	1 (1)	1 (3)		4	3	4
District of Columbia		(1)	(1)	(2)	2	3 (2)		3	8
Totals:	(1)	(3)	1 (17)	3 (9)	13 (12)	22 (12)	10 (1)	51 (3)	61 (2)

* Senior status judges are indicated in parentheses.

elections."[20] Table 1.1 shows the number of judges named by each president from FDR to Reagan.[21]

About forty to fifty vacancies now occur annually on the federal bench, due both to judges taking senior status and to growing caseloads that prompt congressional authorization of new judgeships. Occasionally, Congress also passes omnibus legislation creating a large number of new judgeships at once, such as the Omnibus Judgeship Act of 1978, which created 152 new judgeships. As a result, in 1987 alone, Reagan had the opportunity to make between fifty and seventy-five new appointments. One consequence is that the federal bench may come to bear the imprint of a particular president. Table 1.2 shows the number of sitting judges (and those on senior status) on the courts of appeals in 1986, according to presidential appointment.[22] Republican presidents have appointed 58 percent of the bench; Reagan alone has named over 38 percent. These judges tend to identify with the Republican party, as indicated in Table 1.3.

Table 1.3

**Sitting Judges on the Courts of Appeals and
Party Identifications in 1986***

Circuit	Democrats	Republicans	Independents
First	3	3 (1)	
Second	3 (1)	8 (3)	1
Third	4 (1)	8 (3)	
Fourth	7 (1)	4 (3)	
Fifth	5 (3)	6 (3)	3
Sixth	5 (5)	10 (2)	1
Seventh	2 (2)	9 (2)	
Eighth	4 (1)	5 (1)	
Ninth	11 (1)	12 (5)	1
Tenth	3 (3)	4 (2)	1
Eleventh	3 (4)	6 (2)	3
Federal	2 (4)	8 (1)	3
District of Columbia	3 (3)	8 (3)	2
Totals:	55 (29)	91 (31)	15

* Senior status judges are indicated in parentheses.

Table 1.4 shows that much the same is true for the federal district courts. Republican presidents made 57 percent of the appointments (64 percent of those were made by Reagan). These judges also overwhelmingly identify with the Republican party.

Table 1.4

Presidential Appointments and Judges
on the Federal District Courts in 1986

Judges

Truman	3
Eisenhower	2
Kennedy	5
Johnson	30
Nixon	67
Ford	42
Carter	192
Reagan	203

The growing number of judicial appointments and their greater political significance underscore the fact that the Senate has an increasingly important role to play in scrutinizing nominees—a role that becomes larger and more difficult each year. As Republican Senator Orrin Hatch has commented, the routine processing of nominations is "simply inappropriate when an entire branch of the national government is literally being refashioned over a period of months."[23]

The Presidential Imprint on Judicial Policymaking

Both liberals and conservatives agree that judgeships are an instrument for achieving legal-policy goals. According to Bruce Fein, a former associate deputy attorney general in the Reagan administration, "the judiciary is a primary player in the formulation of public policy."[24] There is disagreement, however, on whether this will prove pernicious or auspicious for the administration of justice and national public law and policy.

Liberal organizations—People for the American Way, the NAACP Legal Defense Fund, and the Alliance for Justice (representing a number of groups), among others—charge that Reagan has imposed a rigid ideological view on the judiciary. One critic, law school professor Herman Schwartz, says the Reagan administration is bent on "turning the federal courts away from their historic role of protecting individual rights [and] this effort will politicize the courts and deprive them of both the substance and the appearance of that fairness on which so much of their legitimacy depends."[25]

By contrast, conservative groups—the Center for Judicial Studies, the Heritage Foundation, and the Washington Legal Foundation among them—applaud the Reagan administration's endeavor to redefine the role of the judiciary. They pressure those in the Department of Justice and close to the president to keep "his pledge to appoint men and women to the bench who exercise restraint."[26]

Both liberals and conservatives are concerned about whether Reagan's judges adhere to his administration's legal-policy goals. In a study of sixty-two of Reagan's initial appointees, Craig Stern of the Center for Judicial Studies concludes:

> Of the sixty-two judges evaluated in this study under the standards specified [i.e., adherence to the 1980 Republican platform] thirty-one judges exercised restraint in all of their significant cases without exception . . . sixteen exercised restraint in no more than half of their significant cases . . . and six published no [pertinent] opinions. . . . The conclusion is inescapable that the Reagan judiciary, so far, has lived up to expectations.[27]

In the view of James McClellan, founder of the Center for Judicial Studies and a former aide to Senators Hatch and Jesse Helms, "the President has done exceedingly well at the appellate level and fairly well at the district level."[28] While such claims fuel debate, there is little empirical evidence on whether—or how significantly—the judiciary has changed or what direction it will take in the future. And conclusions drawn from available data now are at best preliminary and tentative.

Some studies suggest that judicial ideology is significant in less than one case out of six and that partisan considerations—like party affiliation—explain only a fraction of all rulings.[29] In a study of the voting behavior of courts of appeals judges during 1983-84, Jon Gottschall found that in nonunanimous cases involving civil rights and liberties, "appointees of the Carter and the Kennedy/Johnson administrations cast, respectively, 63 percent and 61 percent of their votes for the liberal result, whereas the Reagan and Nixon/Ford appointees both cast only 26 percent of their votes in favor of what has been defined as the liberal outcome." At the same time, Carter and Reagan appointees agreed in 74 percent of the cases in which they participated together. When they disagreed, though, their differences were profound. Gottschall found that "Carter appointees voted for what has been defined as the liberal outcome 95 percent of the time, as compared to 5 percent for the Reagan appointees." Yet contrary to claims of both liberal critics and conservative supporters of the administration, Gottschall found that judges appointed by Reagan were no more partisan than those appointed by Nixon and Ford.[30]

A more comprehensive study, focusing on criminal justice rulings in district and appellate courts during 1981-84, by C. K. Rowland, Donald Songer, and Robert Carp, reveals a sharper divergence between Reagan judges and those of other administrations. The differences were statistically significant at the level of district courts and still greater at the appellate court level. These political scientists found that Carter's district court judges are 64 percent more favorably disposed toward claims made by criminal defendants than are Reagan's judges. And Carter's appellate judges "are almost 90 percent more likely than Reagan appointees to support the criminal defendant." When the voting of Reagan's appellate judges is compared with that of the remaining Nixon appointees, Nixon's judges are found to be more moderate and less politically aligned than indicated by Gottschall's study. As Rowland, Songer, and Carp conclude, "Nixon appointees actually [are] somewhat more supportive of criminal defendants, while Carter appointees become dramatically more supportive and Reagan appointees slightly less supportive."[31] Their evidence supports the view that changes in the politics of appointments may shift the direction of judicial policymaking.

Conclusion: The Policy Debate over Judicial Appointments

Debate over judicial selection is as old as the Constitution. It is a debate over political partisanship and ideology, judicial independence and accountability. During the summer of 1986, with Ronald Reagan's nomination—and the subsequent confirmation—of William Rehnquist as chief justice and Antonin Scalia as associate justice of the Supreme Court, the debate intensified. It loomed even larger with the bitter battles over Reagan's two unsuccessful nominations—Judges Robert H. Bork and Douglas H. Ginsburg—to the seat vacated by Justice Lewis F. Powell, Jr., in 1987. And even after the Senate's unanimous confirmation of Judge Anthony M. Kennedy in 1988, the debate is certain to continue.

The aim here is to clarify the debate over appointing federal judges by putting the politics of judicial appointments into historical perspective—pointing out the trends and changes from FDR through Reagan as well as the views of the Founding Fathers and how they bear on the politics of judicial appointments; by considering arguments for merit selection as well as for geographic, religious, racial, gender, and ethnic representation on the bench; and by examining the roles of the Senate and the American Bar Association in the quest for high-quality appointments.

The changing role of the courts and composition of the federal bench makes a fresh look at judicial appointments critical at this time. For the judiciary has the power to maintain continuity or to forge change in our legal and social policy, and in so doing profoundly affect the management of public affairs.

· 2 ·

Politics and Judgeships

AS WITH MUCH ELSE, the Constitutional Convention in 1787 had to compromise on the process of appointing federal judges. Then, as now, opinion was divided over how to accommodate competing demands for judicial independence from those who appointed the judges and accountability to the public. The debates among the Founding Fathers culminated in giving the president the power to nominate and—with the advice and consent of the Senate—appoint members of the Supreme Court. As to lower federal court judges, the Constitution was—and remains—sufficiently ambiguous as to allow for a variety of options in making judicial appointments. In any event, partisan politics quickly came to control the appointment of all federal judges. As a result, the judiciary falls short of being either a meritocracy or representative of the American electorate.

The Appointment Power and the Founding Fathers

One of the grievances against the King, cited by Thomas Jefferson in the Declaration of Independence, was that "he has made judges dependent upon his will alone for the tenure of their offices and the amount and payment of their salaries."[1] But though judicial independence was deemed important, there were those—like the anti-Federalists—who, out of concern for state and local interests, pushed for popular accountability of judges. (More recent court reformers and critics argue for accountability in terms of gaining direct representation of the electorate on the federal bench.)[2]

Circumstances conspired to have the president and the Senate share the appointment power. Initially, the delegates at Philadelphia considered the Virginia Plan, which gave Congress the power to choose an executive and members of the federal judiciary. Pennsylvania's delegate James

Wilson objected, arguing that "experience showed the impropriety of such appointments by numerous bodies. Intrigue, partiality, and concealment were the necessary consequences." He believed that vesting power in the executive—"a single responsible person"—was more prudent. John Rutledge of South Carolina was not "disposed to grant so great a power to any single person. The people will think that we are leaning too much toward Monarchy."[3]

James Madison sought compromise. He did not favor congressional control: "Beside the danger of intrigue and partiality, many of the members [of legislatures] were not judges of the requisite qualifications. The Legislative talents, which were very different from those of a Judge, commonly recommend men to the favor of Legislative Assemblies." But neither was he inclined to give complete control to the executive. He proposed and won tentative agreement on giving the appointment power to the Senate.

Agreement proved elusive. The New Jersey Plan, which provided for appointments by an executive who was elected by the legislature, was put forward by William Paterson. During debate over this proposal, the leading advocate of a strong executive, Alexander Hamilton, suggested that judges "be appointed or nominated by the Executive to the Senate, which should have the right of rejection or approving." This was the first suggestion of the method that would eventually find its way into the Constitution. At the time, though, the proposal failed to command support.

A month passed before the next debate. It arose over a resolution "that a national judiciary be established to consist of one supreme tribunal the judges of which [shall] be appointed by the second branch of the National Legislature." Massachusetts's Nathaniel Gorham objected on the grounds that the Senate was too numerous "and too little personally responsible, to ensure a good choice." He favored appointments by the executive with the advice and consent of the Senate. Wilson moved to lodge the power in the executive, but that failed by a vote of two to six; Gorham lost on a tie vote.

Madison put forth still another compromise. He called for appointments by the president, subject to disapproval by two-thirds of the Senate. A vote on the measure was postponed; it never actually was taken, as Madison again modified his resolution. He unsuccessfully proposed that only a simple majority of the Senate need reject a nomination. That proposal lost by a vote of three to six, but the provision for senatorial appointment was retained.

Not until early September, almost three months later, when the Special Committee on Postponed Matters made its report, was the issue further debated. The committee proposed that "the President shall nominate, and by and with the advice and consent of the Senate, shall appoint Ambassadors, and other public Ministers, Judges of the Supreme Court, and all other Officers of the U.S., whose appointments are not otherwise herein provided for." After debate, the provision was amended to authorize the president to make recess appointments—appointments made when Congress is not in session—and then adopted. One final change came on the next to the last day of the Convention, when Gouverneur Morris won support for adding the clause, "but Congress may by law vest the appointment of such inferior officers as they think proper in the President alone, in the Courts of Law, or in the heads of Departments."[4]

There was little subsequent debate in the state conventions when ratifying the Constitution. The anti-Federalists' fears about the national government focused some attention on the potential for presidents to conspire with senators. But in most state conventions the primary concern was that the Senate might have too much influence.

Defenders of the Constitution sought to allay these concerns.[5] The strongest defense of the appointment process was offered by Alexander Hamilton in *The Federalist*:

It will be the office of the President to NOMINATE, and with the advice and consent of the Senate to APPOINT. There will, of course, be exertion of CHOICE on the part of the Senate. They may defeat one choice of the Executive and oblige him to make another; but they cannot themselves CHOOSE—they can only ratify or reject the choice of the President. They might even entertain a preference to some other person, at the very moment they were assenting to the one proposed, because there might be no positive ground of opposition to him; and they could not be sure, if they withheld their assent, that the subsequent nomination would fall upon their own favorite, or upon any other person in their estimation more meritorious than the one rejected. Thus it could hardly happen that the majority of the Senate would feel any other complacency toward the object of an appointment than such as the appearances of merit might inspire, and the proofs of the want of it destroy.[6]

Hamilton perceived the president's power to nominate and the power to appoint as one and the same. "It is not easy to conceive a plan better calculated than this to promote a judicious choice of men for filling the offices of the Union," he later claimed, though adding that "must essentially depend [on] the character of its administration." He viewed senatorial participation as potentially pernicious:

> The intrinsic merit of the candidate will be too often out of sight. . . . The coalition will commonly turn upon some interested equivalent: "Give us the man we wish for this office, and you shall have the one you wish for that." This will be the usual condition of the bargain. And it will rarely happen that the advancement of the public service will be the primary object either of the party victories or of party negotiations.[7]

Although the views of Hamilton and other Federalists still appeal to those favoring a presidential prerogative in naming federal judges, they failed to prove persuasive for very long after George Washington's administration.[8] While the Federalists had the final say on the Constitution, as historian Kermit Hall observes, "much as the Antifederalists had wanted, senators, with their local attachments, steadily gained the initiative in the selection of lower court judges."[9] This was due to the rise of political parties, which led to greater partisanship and political patronage.

The Struggle for Power and Political Norms

The compromises struck in the Constitution quickly gave way to partisan struggles. Though Washington sought professionally competent and politically acceptable nominees from various state courts for the bench, the Senate denied him the appointment of a naval officer, Benjamin Fishbourn. In another instance—on the question of John Rutledge becoming chief justice—even Hamilton backed down from his strong position in *The Federalist* that there should be presidential dominance over appointments. In 1795, Hamilton wrote that "if it be really true" that John Rutledge, the nominee for chief justice, "has exposed himself by improper conduct in pecuniary transaction" then he should be rejected. The failure of Rutledge to win confirmation on his elevation from associate to chief justice was the first of twelve nominations to the Supreme Court defeated outright by the Senate. Another eight nominations were withdrawn, and eight more nominations failed because the Senate either took no action or indefinitely postponed action.[10] (See Chapter 4; especially Table 4.1.)

The Senate greatly expanded its influence during the presidency of John Adams. Divisions between the Federalists (associated with Adams and Hamilton) and the Republicans (linked with Jefferson and Madison) led to the first major partisan effort to pack the bench in 1800. Following Jefferson's election, a lame-duck Federalist Congress passed the Judiciary Act of 1801, creating new judgeships and the opportunity to secure a judiciary dominated by Federalists. The Jeffersonian Republicans retaliated by repealing the act.

Almost from the outset of the Republic, judgeships were the object of partisan patronage. Since 1800, the Senate has gradually asserted more power, though the extent of its influence depended (and continues to depend) on the strength of each president. By the 1840s, senatorial courtesy was established, giving senators a virtually absolute veto power over judicial appointments in their home states.

The conferring of lower-court judgeships remains a matter of partisan politics. At the turn of the century, President Theodore Roosevelt, trying to make the best of it, commented that "the Senators and Congressmen shall ordinarily name the man, but I shall name the *standard;* and the men have got to come up to it."[11] In 1931, Burke Shartel offered a more critical view of the prevailing practice: "The fact that inferior judgeships are treated as 'party pie' is not the worst of it. Worse is the fact that these judgeships have become local 'party pie.' District and circuit judgeships have come to be regarded as jobs to be handed out at the behest of the local party chiefs. The President has almost abdicated his power of selection."[12]

The appointment process evolved in the nineteenth century into a bargaining process in which the Senate's influence is greater over lower federal court judgeships and that of the president over appointees to the Supreme Court. Presidents trade lower-court judgeships for legislation and good relations. As a result, for district courts, in former Attorney General Robert F. Kennedy's words, "Basically, it's senatorial appointment with the advice and consent of the Senate."[13] Presidents have greater discretion at the level of circuit courts of appeals, whose jurisdiction spans several states. They may play senators off against each other, claiming that representation from different political parties, geographical regions, religions, races, and so forth is needed. "In the case of the Supreme Court Justices," William Mitchell, President Herbert Hoover's attorney general, observed, "with the whole country to choose from, the Senators from one state or another are in no position even if they were so inclined, to attempt a controlling influence. Such an appointment is not a local matter, and the entire nation has an equal interest and responsibility."[14] Still, the Senate as a whole has the power to influence the selection of—and even to defeat—a president's nominee.

Because of partisan politics and the ambiguity of Article II, section 2 of the Constitution, the role of the Senate in judicial selection is far greater than envisioned by the Founding Fathers. Yet, the language of Article II allows for several methods of appointing lower-court judges. It provides that the president "shall nominate, and by and with the Advice and Consent of the Senate, shall appoint . . . Judges of the Supreme Court, and other Officers of the United States, whose Appointments are not herein otherwise provided for, and which shall be established by law. . . ." But it also states that "Congress may by Law vest the Appointment of such inferior Officers, as they think proper, in the President alone, in the Courts of Law, or in the Heads of Departments." Based on the latter clause, Shartel and political scientist Harold Chase argue that lower-court judges are "inferior officers"—both in the sense of being judges of courts "lower than" the Supreme Court and in the sense that they are officers of "such inferior Courts as the Congress may from time to time ordain to establish."[15] They conclude, therefore, that Congress could (without amending the Constitution) give the president, the attorney general, the Senate, the Supreme Court, or a judicial selection commission the power to appoint lower-court judges.

Throughout most of our history, lower-court judges were assumed to be simply "inferior officers." Not until the Circuit Courts of Appeals Act of 1891, which created the courts of appeals as we know them today, did Congress specifically provide that "there shall be appointed by the President of the United States, by and with the advice and consent of the Senate, in each circuit an additional circuit judge." Only when the law was recodified in 1948 was it required that all federal judges be appointed by the president with the advice and consent of the Senate.[16]

The judicial appointment process is thus more firmly grounded in political norms than in the Constitution. The possibility of major confrontations undergirds these norms. In the past century, for example, Congress successfully both denied presidents additional appointments (in order to preserve the Court's policies) and increased the number of justices so as to change the ideological composition of the Court. In this century, Congress has withheld authorization of lower-court judgeships as well as approval of nominees so as to deny lame-duck presidents their judicial appointees. It did so in 1960 and, again, in 1975 in order to deny outgoing Presidents Eisenhower and Ford large numbers of lower-court judicial appointments. Because of the Senate's vested interests in district court judgeships, Congress is unlikely to give a president complete control over appointments. Further, were a president to seriously threaten the prevailing norms governing the appointment of lower-court judges, Congress might attempt to take away presidential prerogatives in the appointment of lower-court judges. There is little doubt that such a move could deprive a president of his influence over the appointment of lower-court judges. Congress has circumscribed the president's appointment power in the courts of the District of Columbia. By statute, the District of Columbia Nominating Commission provides the president with a list of candidates for judicial vacancies, and the president must nominate a judge from that list within sixty days. If he fails to do so, the commission may nominate and, with the advice and consent of the Senate, appoint a judge from its list.[17] Disagreements between the commission and the president have, thus far, been resolved—usually through compromise. In one instance, though, in 1986, a potential constitutional conflict was only narrowly avoided. Philip Lacovara, Reagan's representative on the commission, who was reappointed for a second term, decided to resign because of difficulties he had in dealing with the Department of Justice's "ideological litmus test" for judicial candidates.[18]

In sum, the compromise struck in Article II, section 2 provides a basis both for presidents to claim judgeships as a personal prerogative and for Congress to expand or take away presidential patronage in the lower federal courts.

Partisan Politics and Merit

Because partisan politics dominates the selection of judges, presidents make no effort to achieve a political balance in the judiciary. The party affiliations of those who have served on the Supreme Court largely reflect the politics of their presidential benefactors: thirteen Federalists, one Whig, eight Democratic-Republicans, thirty-nine Republicans, and forty-two Democrats.[19] Similarly, statistics show that between 1885 and 1940, almost 95 percent of lower federal court appointments were from members of the party in power.[20] Table 2.1 shows the party affiliations of judges appointed by presidents from FDR to Reagan.[21]

Despite a history of partisan appointments, the myth still circulates that judges should be selected strictly on the basis of merit. Attorney

General Ramsey Clark, for instance, confided to President Lyndon Johnson, "I think a most significant contribution to American Government would be the non-political appointment of judges."[22] Subsequently, President Carter created—by executive order—so-called merit commissions for the selection of appellate judges and urged senators to do the same for district court judges. Still, Johnson's and Carter's appointments turned on politics, as have those of all other presidents.

The basic fact remains that every appointment is political and the judiciary is not a meritocracy. This is so because of the difficulty of defining merit and because of the politics of judicial selection.

Any definition of "judicial merit" is artificial. Henry Abraham, a leading scholar on the appointment of justices, proposed the following criteria: demonstrated judicial temperament; professional expertise and competence; absolute personal and professional integrity; an able, agile, lucid mind; appropriate professional educational background or training; and the ability to communicate clearly, both orally and in writing.[23] Yet, justices themselves have difficulty in defining such qualities as "judicial temperament."[24] Judicial merit is perhaps reducible only to the standard of "obscenity" offered by Justice Potter Stewart: "I know it when I see it."[25]

Definitions of judicial merit, at best, set forth the *minimum qualifications*. Walter Schaefer, a former chief justice of the Supreme Court of Illinois, expressed the point when observing that:

> To me the qualifications for a judge, as they are ordinarily expressed, are quite unsatisfactory. He must have, it is often said, legal ability, a judicial temperament, and integrity. . . . As standards these qualifications . . . are hopelessly minimal. They operate only upon surface factors. And without rather elaborate tacit footnotes their strict observance could produce a very mediocre bench.[26]

Edward J. Devitt, another respected judge on a federal district court, cautioned about overemphasizing merit:

> I doubt if federal judges ever will be appointed solely on the basis of merit. That would be the millennium. So long as the United States Senate has the constitutionally granted authority to "advise and consent" to such appointments, it is unlikely that some politics will not be involved in most of them. The truth remains . . . that we were appointed to office because, personally or vicariously, we knew the United States senators; and that, I emphasize, is not a sinful thing at all.[27]

Table 2.1

Party Affiliation of Judges Appointed
by Presidents from FDR to Reagan

President	Party	Appointees from Same Party
Roosevelt	Democrat	97%
Truman	Democrat	92%
Eisenhower	Republican	95%
Kennedy	Democrat	92%
Johnson	Democrat	94%
Nixon	Republican	93%
Ford	Republican	81%
Carter	Democrat	90%
Reagan	Republican	97%

Griffin Bell, a former federal judge who later as attorney general oversaw Carter's judicial appointments, is candid about the politics of judicial selection. "Becoming a federal judge wasn't very difficult," he recalls of his own appointment. "I managed John F. Kennedy's presidential campaign in Georgia. Two of my oldest friends were the senators from Georgia. And I was campaign manager and special counsel for the governor."[28]

Because of the difficulty of defining and applying standards of judicial merit and because the selection of judges is based in politics, the appointment of judges, as Justice Harlan F. Stone put it, is like a "lottery." As a result, meritorious individuals are passed over for the Supreme Court as well as for lower courts. Benjamin Cardozo, for one, was repeatedly passed over until circumstances conspired to make his appointment opportune. Judge Learned Hand later lost out altogether, as did Paul Freund, a respected Harvard Law School professor who was considered but denied a seat on the high bench by Presidents Kennedy, Johnson, and Ford.[29]

Circumstances and chance political associations loom no less in the selection of lower federal court judges. Based on interviews with circuit judges, political scientist J. Woodford Howard finds that judges themselves consider "political participation, professional competence, personal ambition, plus an oft-mentioned pinch of luck" responsible for their appointments.[30] Similarly, Donald Jackson, another student of judicial politics, observes that "federal judges are chosen by a sort of political roulette. The participants in the process are constant—senators, perhaps a congressman, the Justice Department, the President, campaigning candidates, the ABA—but their relative strength varies with the individual cases. Each selection is a fresh spin of the wheel." As a result, Jackson concludes, "federal judges are an elite, but in a special sense: not an aristocracy of intellect and ability, but rather the cream of the partisans, the best of the political scramblers."[31]

It bears emphasizing that the pool from which all judges are drawn is by no means representative of the country. To the contrary, the boundaries that restrict the pool of potential candidates are tightly drawn, and chance or luck comes to play only in the final stages of making selections. As Howard puts it, "the passage from the sea of eligibles to the narrow channels of candidacy . . . requires luck. This usually meant a chance convergence of basic credentials with the politics of final selection—knowing the right people at the right time."[32] Party affiliation, however, remains a critical consideration. During any presidency—whether Democratic or Republican—potential candidates identified with the party out of power are virtually excluded from the pool of candidates given serious consideration.

Courts and Representation

The federal judiciary was not designed to be a representative institution, though in recent years—particularly during the Carter administration—liberals and judicial reformers have sought to make it so. Educational background and socioeconomic considerations, no less than partisan politics, work to make it a bastion of upper-middle- to upper-class white Anglo-Saxon Protestant males.

A collective portrait of those who have served on the bench is provided by political scientist John Schmidhauser in his study of justices and judges:

> Throughout American history there has been an overwhelming tendency for presidents to choose nominees for the Supreme Court from among the socially advantaged families. The typical Supreme Court justice has generally been white, Protestant (with a penchant for a high social status denomination), usually of ethnic stock originating in the British Isles, and born in comfortable circumstances in an urban or small-town environment. In the earlier history of the Court, he tended to come from

the professionalized upper middle class. While nearly two-thirds of his fellows were selected from politically active families having a tradition of judicial service. In college and legal education, the average justice was afforded very advantageous opportunities for training and associations. . . .Very few sons of families outside the upper or upper-middle social economic classes have been able to acquire the particular type of education and the subsequent professional and especially political associations which appear to be unwritten prerequisites for appointment to the nation's highest tribunal.

The collective portrait of the Courts of Appeal judges is very similar, but with less emphasis on political and judicial family background, especially after the Civil War, less emphasis on personal political participation, less emphasis on high-status legal education, but greater emphasis on prior judicial experience and a bit more upon Bar Association activity and membership.[33]

Supreme Court justices and judges are disproportionately selected from prominent positions in the legal profession, the executive branch, and lower federal and state courts. The prior positions of the 104 justices who have served on the Supreme Court are shown in Table 2.2.

The same may be said for lower-court judges, who traditionally have been white male lawyers from upper-middle-class backgrounds with good political connections. Moreover, even the occasional black, woman, or ethnic judge tends to come from among the socially and politically ad-

Table 2.2

Prior Occupations of Justices of the Supreme Court of the United States

Prior Occupations	Number of Justices
Private legal practice	25
Federal bench	23
Executive branch	21
State bench	21
U.S. Senate	6
State governorship	3
House of Representatives	2
Law school professor	2
Miscellaneous	1

vantaged. The underrepresentation of these segments of the population on the bench reflects both career patterns and the recruitment policies of administrations.

For most of our history, race, religion, gender, and ethnicity have been barriers to judicial appointment. Tables 2.3 and 2.4 show the total number of blacks and women who have served on the federal bench, by court and by appointing president.[34]

Until twenty-five years ago, educational opportunities were not available to significant numbers of blacks. According to political scientist Thomas Uhlman, "Only in the mid-to-late 1960s did legal training at the predominantly white institution become a realistic possibility for American blacks."[35] The American Bar Association excluded blacks from

Table 2.3

Number of Black Judges Appointed by Presidents from FDR to Reagan*

Court	Number of Judges	Appointing President
Supreme Court	1	Johnson
Courts of Appeals	1	Truman
	1	Kennedy
	2	Johnson
	9	Carter
	1	Reagan
District Courts	3	Kennedy
	5	Johnson
	6	Nixon
	3	Ford
	28	Carter
	4	Reagan
Special Courts	1	Johnson
	1	Eisenhower
Total:	66	

*Nine of these black judges were women. One was appointed by Johnson, seven by Carter, and one by Reagan.

Table 2.4

Number of Women Judges
Appointed to the Federal Bench

Court	Number of Judges	Appointing President
Supreme Court	1	Reagan
Courts of Appeals	1	Roosevelt
	1	Johnson
	11	Carter
	6	Reagan*
District Courts	1	Truman
	1	Kennedy
	2	Johnson
	1	Nixon
	1	Ford
	29	Carter
	22	Reagan*
Special Courts	1	Coolidge
	1	Eisenhower
	1	Carter
	1	Reagan
Total:	81	

*Reagan appointed two women to the district courts and subsequently elevated them to the appellate bench. They are counted here only as appointments to the courts of appeals.

its ranks until the early part of this century, and thereafter provided little support for black attorneys who sought to advance their careers.

Opportunities for women on the federal bench opened up earlier than for blacks and other ethnic groups. Still, women did not make significant gains in entering the practice of law or in reaching the federal bench until the past decade. Although in the late nineteenth century women law school graduates won admission to legal practice with greater frequency, by 1910, they still constituted only 1 percent of all lawyers. Little changed over the years. Women made up only 2.1 percent of the legal profession in 1930 and only 2.8 percent four decades later in 1970.

In the 1970s, the number of women entering the legal profession increased dramatically. By 1980, women constituted approximately 13 percent of the profession, and if current trends continue nearly one-third of all lawyers will be women by the year 2000.[36] In spite of this, sociologist Cynthia Epstein finds that women remain underrepresented in large corporate law firms—particularly at the level of partner, from which males tend to be recruited for the federal bench.[37] Consequently, when administrations have sought women for judgeships, they have tended to turn to those teaching at law schools. Women now make up not quite 8 percent of the judiciary, and that is due to a great extent to Carter appointments.

Blacks and women who have made it to the federal bench have done so by traveling paths quite different from that of their white male counterparts. As political scientist Elliot Slotnick finds in a study of Carter's appointments to the lower federal courts:

> White male candidates were generally recruited for judgeships after having travelled a well worn path established by a time honored selection process. They enjoyed long years of legal experience, prestigious courtroom admissions and, for the most part, highly successful private practices. Such prominent and successful private practices were not likely to be fertile grounds for locating viable non-traditional judgeship candidates. Non-whites, however, were recruited from sitting judgeships or, more generally, from among those who had gained some public prominence in their legal careers through their judicial experience. Non-whites, particularly males, were most likely to have had legal aid backgrounds and to have served in predominantly criminal practices. . . . In seeking women for the bench, recruitment authorities turned disproportionately to the law schools where several women attorneys had gained prominence as academicians.[38]

It remains to be seen whether the composition of the federal judiciary will change along with the legal profession.

Administrations' recruitment policies are no less important in determining the makeup of the federal bench. This has especially been the case in the past decade (1976-86) when the pool of black and women lawyers and state judges grew markedly.

The major change in the composition of the federal bench was a product of the Carter administration's affirmative action policy. "By the end of the Carter administration," political scientist Sheldon Goldman observes, "the proportion of women judges on the federal bench had risen from one per cent to close to seven per cent and, for blacks, from four per cent to close to nine per cent."[39] Blacks made up 13.5 percent of the district court judges named by Carter (28 out of 206), and 16 percent of his appellate court judges were black. Almost 20 percent of Carter's appointees to appellate courts and 14.4 percent of his appointees at the district level were women.

While the Carter administration's quest for a more representative judiciary remains controversial, the appointment of more women, blacks, or other minorities does not indicate major changes in judicial policymaking. Greater representation of these groups on the federal bench is largely a matter of symbolic politics. Women, blacks, Catholics, Jews, and members of other ethnic groups do not hold a single view on statutory interpretation, for example, or agree on such divisive legal-policy issues as abortion or school prayer. Further, those who make it to the bench have internalized the old norms and practices of the legal profession. As Beverly Cook noted in a study of women trial court judges:

> There is little room even for the brilliant woman to effect major changes in procedure and policies. Her career security depends on her general acceptance of the old norms. . . . Those identified as deviants in any way except gender are vulnerable to criticism and removal from power. Challenges to the culture are somewhat easier (although less likely) from those who fit the stereotype of ascriptions. Women judges probably can not make major changes in policy outputs.[40]

The same is true of black judges.[41] There is little empirical evidence to suggest that the voting behavior of black judges diverges from that of white judges—at least in ways other than those associated with party identification.

There has been widespread criticism that black and women judges with lesser qualifications were appointed over more qualified white males. Based on studies of Carter appointees, it seems fair to say that "merit" was not compromised or sacrificed (at least not to any greater degree than it was by other administrations). As Goldman concludes, "the women and minorities chosen by the Carter Administration on the whole may even be more distinguished than the overall credentials of the white males chosen by Carter and previous administrations."[42]

Another criticism—and one championed by the Reagan administration —is that such "representative" considerations are irrelevant and pernicious in the appointment of judges. Yet such "representative" considerations as geography, religion, race, gender, and ethnicity have long had a role in the politics of appointing judges.

Political Trade-Offs and
Demands for a Representative Judiciary

Packing the federal bench has long meant more than filling it with party faithful and ideological kin. Since the administration of George Washington, demands for other kinds of representation have had to be accommodated too. The kinds of representation demanded—and achieved—ebb and flow with social and political forces within the country.

Geography. Geography once figured prominently in appointments to the Supreme Court. During the nineteenth century, geographic representation—aimed at assuring respect for the distinctive cultural values of different regions—was considered critical to establishing the legitimacy of the judiciary and the national government.

Congress encouraged geographical representation by requiring the justices to ride circuit. From the appointment of John Rutledge from South Carolina in 1789 until the retirement of Hugo Black from Alabama in 1971—with the exception of the Reconstruction decade (1865-76)—there was always a southerner on the Supreme Court. Until 1867, the sixth seat was reserved as the "southern seat." Until Benjamin Cardozo's appointment in 1932, the third seat was reserved for New Englanders.

As the country expanded westward, presidents gave representation to new states and regions. After the Civil War, the influx of immigrants diminished the importance of geographical regions as did Congress's elimination of circuit riding in 1891.

A few Supreme Court appointments in this century turned on geography. President William Howard Taft, for example, selected Willis Van Devanter from Wyoming in 1910 because he was determined to have a westerner. After Taft became chief justice, he continued to lobby presidents Warren Harding and Calvin Coolidge for geographical balance on the Court. Roosevelt's picking of midwesterner Wiley Rutledge in 1943 was perhaps the last time that geography figured prominently in an appointment to the Court. Even then, FDR gave eight others appointments before turning to Rutledge.[43]

Since then, the attempt to achieve geographic representation has declined. When Black was still on the bench, Clement F. Haynsworth, Jr., of South Carolina and G. Harrold Carswell of Florida were nominated by Richard Nixon because, he claimed, southerners "deserve representation on the Court." But after the Senate rejected both nominees, Nixon did not let geography stand in the way of naming Harry Blackmun from Minnesota—even though his earlier appointee, Warren Burger, was from that state. Nor did geography stop Reagan from appointing William Rehnquist's former law school classmate Sandra Day O'Connor—though both were from Arizona.

Geographic diversity remains important in the selection of appellate court judges. Within a circuit, balance is usually sought on the basis of population, caseloads, and the number of judges from different states within a circuit.[44] At the level of district courts, geography is controlling. Traditionally, the nominee must be a resident of the state and the district in which a vacancy occurs; it is almost impossible to get a nonresident through the Senate confirmation process.

Religion. Religion has generally been a barrier to, rather than a basis for, judicial appointment. The overwhelming majority (91) of the 104 Supreme Court justices have been of the Protestant faith. Of the remaining twelve, eight were Catholics and five were Jews.

Religous representation was not an issue in judicial selection until almost the mid-twentieth century. But as geographic representation became less critical, demographic considerations began to figure more prominently in the appointment process. Eisenhower, for example, sought "a very good Catholic, even a Conservative Democrat," when appointing Justice William J. Brennan in 1956, in order to "show that we mean our declaration that the Court should be nonpartisan."[45]

Still, although politically symbolic, religious representation has not figured as strongly as ideological compatibility with the president. When Reagan named a Catholic, Antonin Scalia, for instance, religion was subordinate to his ideological kinship with the Reagan administration. And he subsequently named another, Anthony M. Kennedy. Again, though, religion did not enter into his selection. Simply put, there has never been a quota system.

Much the same has been true for religious representation on the lower courts. Throughout the past century, there have been few Jewish or Catholic judges. Prior to 1933, less than 8 percent of the judges sitting on the lower federal bench were Catholic or Jewish. The Roosevelt administration made an unprecedented effort to name more non-Protestants. Between 1933 and 1976, the percentage of Catholic and Jewish judges more than doubled.[46]

The religious affiliation of judges appointed by presidents from FDR to Reagan is shown in Table 2.5.[47] Notably, Democratic presidents have appointed more non-Protestants than have Republican presidents. Since the Eisenhower administration, 24.8 percent of the judges named by Democratic presidents have been Catholic, 13.7 percent Jewish; Republicans have filled seats with Catholics less than 18 percent of the time, Jews less than 10 percent of the time.

Overall, religious affiliation has not loomed large in the politics of judicial selection since the Roosevelt/Truman administration. FDR had a virtual "affirmative action policy." His Department of Justice kept detailed records of the Catholic and Jewish vote in various states and made a conscious effort to reward them when appointing judges.[48] The Eisenhower administration remained sensitive to religious affiliations of nominees, but made less of an effort to appoint non-Protestants. The Kennedy administration was wary about being publicly perceived to give too many judgeships to Catholics and Jews.[49] Subsequent administrations have paid less and less attention to recruiting non-Protestant judges.

Race, Gender, and Ethnicity. Democratic presidents have tended (as shown in Tables 2.3 and 2.4) to appoint more women, blacks, and other minorities than have Republicans. Truman named the first black, William Hastie, in 1949; Kennedy then appointed Thurgood Marshall in 1961, and Johnson appointed Wade McCree, Jr., and Spottswood Robinson III in 1966 to the appellate bench. Nixon appointed the first Asian, Herbert Y. C. Choy of Hawaii, a friend and former law partner of that state's Senator Hiram Fong.

Such nontraditional appointments reflect both demographic changes in the voting population and how presidents use judgeships in politically symbolic ways—ways that signify their own political agenda and ostensibly infuse democratic values into the judiciary.

In 1967, for example, Johnson's advisers told him the time had come for the appointment of a black to the Supreme Court, and it was then that Thurgood Marshall was named. Marshall had gained national recognition when, as director of the NAACP Counsel of Legal Defense and Education Fund, he had argued *Brown v. Board of Education* in 1954. In 1961, Kennedy named Marshall to the Court of Appeals for

Table 2.5

Religious Affiliation of Lower-Court Judges
Appointed by Presidents from FDR to Reagan

Religion	FDR	Truman	Eisenhower	Kennedy	Johnson	Nixon	Ford	Carter	Reagan
Protestant	70.9%	59.1%	78.2%	58.9%	58.0%	72.8%	70.3%	59.3%	62.5%
Catholic	24.5%	29.9%	15.8%	30.7%	30.2%	18.3%	20.3%	26.7%	29.2%
Jewish	4.5%	9.4%	5.8%	10.4%	11.7%	8.9%	4.4%	14.0%	8.3%
Totals:	99.9%	98.4%	99.8%	100.0%	99.9%	100.0%	95.0%	100.0%	100.0%

the Second Circuit. Subsequently, Johnson persuaded him to become his solicitor general. Johnson wanted "that image, number one," of having a black solicitor general, Marshall recalls. Johnson had told him, "You know this has nothing to do with any Supreme Court appointment. I want that distinctly understood. There's no quid pro [sic] here at all." But that, of course, was not all there was to it. The solicitor general is in a strategic position for elevation to the Court.[50]

With the battle over the Equal Rights Amendment in the 1970s, pressure also mounted for the appointment of a woman to the Supreme Court. During the Truman administration, Court of Appeals Judge Florence Allen had been mentioned for an appointment. Nixon also considered nominating a woman. But he claimed "that in general the women judges and lawyers qualified to be nominated for the Supreme Court were too liberal to meet the strict constructionist criterion" he had set for appointees.[51] Nixon submitted the name of State Judge Mildred Lillie to the American Bar Association judiciary committee in 1971, but she was ranked as "not qualified." Subsequently, Ford's advisers compiled a list of over twenty women—including Sandra Day O'Connor—for the vacancy created by the retirement of Justice Douglas. During the 1980 election, Reagan made a campaign promise to appoint a woman. Less than a year later, he fulfilled that pledge by naming O'Connor.

Conclusion: The Politics of Judgeships

Partisan politics dominates judicial appointments. The swing of presidential elections largely determines who makes it to the bench. Still, the president and the Senate share power and compete for influence in the appointment process. And from that competition has emerged a set of norms that define the limits of political patronage and structure selection and confirmation. As a result, the judiciary is neither a meritocracy nor expressly representative of the American public.

· 3 ·

Presidential Trends
in Judicial Selection

H ISTORICALLY, presidents have claimed judgeships as a personal prerogative, but they have always competed with senatorial patronage. The days are long gone when presidents appointed lawyers they knew, after consultation and bargaining with senators over their preferences. By the twentieth century, presidents counted on attorneys general to find nominees acceptable both to them and to the Senate.[1] As political scientist Joel Grossman concluded in a 1965 study, "the choice of a federal judge is the attorney general's to make—provided that he makes it within the framework of the relevant norms of behavior which operate on the selection process" and the criteria set by the president.[2]

Presidents set the criteria for selecting judges. In naming federal judges, each president has tended to weigh differently political patronage, professional qualifications, and legal-policy goals. As historian Rayman Soloman shows in a study of appellate court appointments from Theodore Roosevelt to Franklin Roosevelt, those presidents less concerned with judicial policymaking allow patronage to dominate their appointments.[3] During the presidencies of William Howard Taft and Herbert Hoover, though, professionalism vied with patronage due to concern about curbing the courts and the national government. By contrast, Woodrow Wilson and FDR gave greater weight to candidates' legal-policy views and, to some extent, overrode demands for senatorial patronage. Recent administrations—particularly those of Carter and Reagan—have vigorously pursued their own legal-policy goals through the selection of federal judges. As a result, the screening process has become decidedly more rigorous and ideological.

49

New Deal Judges: The Roosevelt and Truman Administrations

Like all presidents, Franklin Roosevelt favored the party faithful when nominating federal judges. But no less important to FDR was personal friendship and "good politics"—that is, playing ball with those who would help achieve his New Deal policies.

As a result, the professional qualifications of FDR's 126 district court nominees were of secondary importance to him. (The overwhelming Democratic majorities in Congress constrained the appointing of his nominees, particularly in the South.) A majority of FDR's appellate judges lacked prior judicial experience. "By any stretch of the imagination," political scientist Richard Burke notes, "only twelve of his forty-six nominees to the circuit bench could be said to be established jurists and most of these were named for personal or political reasons, not as a recognition of merit."[4]

FDR usually knew who he wanted on the bench. He frequently offered them positions or cut deals with senators without consulting his attorney general. This was so whether he filled seats on the Supreme Court or the lower courts.[5] The degree of FDR's personal involvement in judicial selection, which has not been matched by his successors, bothered those in the Justice Department. When serving as solicitor general, Francis Biddle shared his concern in a letter to Attorney General Robert Jackson: "[This] should not be [FDR's] practice, and I cannot help feeling that he doesn't realize the immense importance to his whole program of these federal judges."[6] Jackson, though, knew that FDR considered judgeships a matter "of personal prestige" and would maneuver to have his way.[7]

What disturbed Biddle and others was that FDR ended up with bad appointments. Earlier administrations let the attorney general recommend nominees after consulting with senators, leading lawyers, and law professors around the country.[8] FDR usually turned to his friends for advice. For example, he consulted with Felix Frankfurter and William O. Douglas both before and after he placed them on the high bench. When Frankfurter was teaching at Harvard Law School, he had law students review the opinions of state or district court judges being considered for vacancies, and he would then advise the president.[9] FDR, however, did not invariably seek such advice or even the approval of bar associations. Jackson recalls, he was "desirous of having the approval of the [local] bar associations, if possible . . . not entirely because he agreed with the bar associations, but [as] a matter of self-protection."[10]

When FDR died in the spring of 1945, Harry Truman continued appointing party faithful. Less skillful in dealing with Congress, he faced more opposition from the Senate Judiciary Committee—both when it was controlled by Republicans (1946-49) and later when Democrats reclaimed the Senate.

One indication of Truman's troubles is that he was the last president to have district court nominees rejected on the Senate floor. In 1950, after Democrats regained the Senate, Truman nominated M. Neil Andrews to a district court in Georgia. But he failed to get the approval of Andrews's home-state Senator Richard Russell, who successfully fought the nomination on the ground that the president had acted "in derogation of the dignity of the Senate and its constitutional powers." Without consulting the home-state senator, Truman also nominated a defeated Democratic gubernatorial candidate for a judgeship in Iowa. This nomination, too, was turned down. A year later, Truman made the same mistake again. After polling local bar organizations, Illinois Senator Paul Douglas recommended three individuals for three district court vacancies. Truman nominated one but substituted two others; they ran afoul of Douglas and the Democratic Senate.[11]

Despite these defeats and three other nominations that never made it out of the Senate Judiciary Committee, Truman's judges were of higher quality than those appointed by FDR. Thirteen of the ninety-eight district judges appointed by Truman had been U.S. attorneys, two had been prominent state judges, twenty-four had significant prior judicial experience (five or more years on the bench), and the remainder were practicing lawyers. Out of the twenty-five circuit judges nominated by Truman, nineteen had significant prior judicial experience.

But the quality of the bench improved for reasons more to do with external pressures than with the internal workings of the Truman administration. Some senators, concerned that the bench was being packed with New Deal Democrats, began to rely on bar associations' opinions of nominees. Also, the American Bar Association was demanding a role; four of Truman's appellate judges were the result of the ABA's campaign.

The Eisenhower Years

The Eisenhower administration brought major changes to judicial recruitment and to the judiciary. Twenty years of uninterrupted Democratic control of the White House left a bench that was over 80 percent Democratic. There was pressure within the Republican party and the ABA for restoring political balance and improving the caliber of nominees.

Eisenhower was committed to securing a political balance on the bench and high-caliber appointments.[12] By the end of his administration, there was a roughly even split on the bench between Democrats and Republicans. It was achieved, however, by giving judgeships to Republican party faithful. The goal of improving the caliber of nominees was advanced by greater ABA involvement and by changes in the Department of Justice. As a nonlawyer, Eisenhower thought that the advice of lawyers was critical, and he placed a high value on prior judicial experience. Also, because of his military career, he was more inclined to delegate responsibility to subordinates. As a result, Eisenhower's judges were more professional than those appointed by FDR, Truman, and some others.[13]

Eisenhower was not personally involved in judicial recruitment. His attorney general, Herbert Brownell, delegated the task to the deputy attorney general, who handled matters with virtually complete freedom from the White House. Both of Eisenhower's deputy attorneys general—William Rogers, who served until 1957 when he succeeded Brownell, and Lawrence Walsh, who filled the position after serving for three years on a federal district court—set high standards. Though favoring Republicans, they focused on the "reputation and experience a lawyer had in his community." They worked closely with the ABA and relied heavily on its reports and those prepared by the Federal Bureau of Investigation. Nominees were rarely interviewed and, if so, only about their willingness to uphold the landmark school desegregation ruling in *Brown v. Board of Education*. The Reagan administration, in contrast, has questioned candidates about such controversial issues as abortion—a practice that Brownell says is "shocking,"[14] since what is important is a nominee's legal reputation, not his or her stands on particular issues of public policy.

The Kennedy and Johnson Administrations

Under John F. Kennedy, judicial selection remained largely a staff operation within the Justice Department. But the Kennedy operation had serious shortcomings. For one thing, it relied on a so-called spotter system—young Democratic lawyers around the country—to find nominees: this proved too ad hoc and unreliable. For another, the ABA had less confidence in the Kennedy administration than it had in that of Eisenhower. Further, problems arose from the inexperience of those in the Kennedy Justice Department in dealing with senators.

In comparison with the Eisenhower administration, the Kennedy administration failed to take a hard line with senators—particularly with the powerful Senate Judiciary Committee Chairman James Eastland. According to Rogers, "of the 106 or so appointments in which I participated, I would state that all but two were presidential (as opposed to senatorial) appointments."[15] By contrast, the view of the Kennedy Justice Department was, in the words of Deputy Attorney General Nicholas deB. Katzenbach, "play ball with the ABA, play ball with the Senate, do the best you can, don't let anyone through who has personally attacked the President."[16]

As a result, Kennedy named judges who ran against his own legal-policy goals in the area of civil liberties/civil rights. As journalist Victor Navasky observed, there was an "absence of any deep, abiding and overriding Kennedy commitment to the integrity and quality of the Southern Judiciary itself."[17] Due to an unwillingness to take on senators and to insist on high standards, no blacks were appointed in the South and far more segregationists were named than during the Eisenhower administration. The most notorious of these was William Cox of Mississippi, Eastland's old college roommate, who after donning judicial robes referred to blacks in his courtroom as "niggers."[18]

Deference to senatorial preferences, some scholars claim, persisted in the Justice Department under President Lyndon Johnson.[19] As a former Senate majority leader, Johnson was sensitive to demands for senatorial courtesy; he himself had held up thirteen of Eisenhower's nominees in order to win a judgeship for one of his friends in Texas. Still, Neil McFeeley, a political scientist and lawyer, persuasively argues that "the Justice Department and the White House in the late Johnson administration made independent judgements on nominees and were not bound by senatorial wishes."[20]

After Kennedy's death, Assistant Deputy Attorney General John Dolan continued to identify possible judicial candidates, with the assistance of John Duffner, a career attorney who handled routine matters from 1962 to 1975; Katzenbach made the major decisions. When Attorney General Robert Kennedy resigned in 1964, Katzenbach assumed his post and Ramsey Clark served as deputy attorney general until he rose to the top of the Justice Department in 1967.

Under Katzenbach and Clark, basic procedures remained the same but more initiative was taken than during the Kennedy years to see to it that nominees shared the administration's legal-policy goals. Clark had an extensive questionnaire for those interviewed about possible nominees that included evaluations of temperament, integrity, experience, and reputation, as well as their general political philosophy and views on defendants' rights. In addition, Clark claims to have "had a rule that a person with a history of neutrality on the race issue is not enough. We've been through so many times [when] a person that had never done anything either way, turn[s] out to be a racist."[21]

The Johnson White House also played a greater role in judicial selection than had the Kennedy administration. John Macy, head of the Civil Service Commission, ran a "merit operation" that included locating and reviewing the backgrounds of potential judicial nominees. Johnson also had a greater interest than Kennedy in judicial appointments; he conferred with trusted aides—among them Jack Valenti, Bill Moyers, and Abe Fortas (even after Fortas took his seat on the Supreme Court)—and he was willing to bargain with senators.[22]

Johnson was not always successful in dealing with the Senate, and some of his nominees were not very good. Initially, he had difficulty because he went ahead with some Kennedy nominees; one, David Rabinovitz from Wisconsin, was withdrawn due to opposition over his qualifications from the ABA and his two home-state senators. In 1965, major controversy arose over two nominees. The first, James P. Coleman, was a former governor of Mississippi and a segregationist; he had the backing of Senator Eastland. Civil rights leaders fought the nomination, but Johnson sent Katzenbach to defend Coleman during the confirmation hearings and he won approval. Johnson failed, though, when he put Francis X. Morrissey up for a judgeship. He did so as a favor to Joseph Kennedy, without consulting the Justice Department. Morrissey was rated unqualified by the ABA; he had gone to an unaccredited law school, twice failed the bar examination, and was denounced by a widely respected federal judge in Massachusetts, Chief Judge Charles Wyzanski, among others. Johnson stood by him until the controversy finally forced Senator Edward M. Kennedy to withdraw support, and Morrissey's nomination died.

As in the Kennedy years, the ABA's relations with the Justice Department were troubled. Along with Morrissey, five other nominees were rated unqualified by the ABA in Johnson's first years in office. After the Morrissey controversy, though, Johnson sought ABA backing for nominations, and the closer relationship that he developed with the ABA strengthened his hand in dealing with senators and in getting his nominees confirmed during his remaining three years in office.

Johnson suffered a major defeat in late 1968, when he proposed elevating Justice Fortas to chief justice upon the retirement of Earl Warren. Johnson overestimated his influence after he had announced that he would not seek reelection. Anticipating Richard Nixon's victory in the presidential election, Republican senators wanted to deny Johnson any appointments to the Court. And Republicans and conservative southern Democrats in the Senate marshaled opposition against Fortas because of his support of the Warren Court's "liberal jurisprudence." After prolonged hearings, Fortas asked to be withdrawn from consideration.

Despite the Fortas controversy, Johnson improved the quality of the bench and pursued his legal-policy goals more successfully than had Kennedy. Still, as McFeeley concludes, "It is doubtful that President Johnson ever brought together the attorney general, Macy, and the White House staff members involved and laid out specific guidelines." Johnson's efforts were unsystematic and lacked "a guiding philosophy behind the judicial selection process."[23] In this, Johnson differed from his successors.

The Nixon Years

As a lawyer, Richard Nixon prided himself on a well-developed judicial philosophy. After a campaign based on returning "law and order" to the country, Nixon promised to name only "strict constructionists" and advocates of judicial self-restraint to the federal bench. He was also the first president to pledge not to nominate anyone—except to the Supreme Court—found "not qualified" by the ABA.

The Nixon administration, however, did not follow through on his pledge to appoint only those sharing Nixon's judicial conservatism. Under attorney general John Mitchell, deputy attorney general Richard Kleindienst assumed responsibility for judicial nominations. He claimed party loyalty would play a "very very minor part,"[24] but failed to counter senatorial patronage.

The administration was not more successful for a number of reasons. At first, it was constrained by a Democratic-controlled Congress; later, the Watergate scandal eroded its negotiating position with the Senate. From the outset, the administration failed to take a hard line with Republican senators. Unless a nominee was rated as "not qualified" by the ABA, it usually acquiesced to Senators' choices; it even bent to liberal

Republicans. Senator Lowell Weicker, for one, got the administration to nominate Governor Thomas Meskill (apparently because he feared a primary election challenge), even though the ABA ranked him as unqualified.[25]

Nixon's interest in judges focused primarily on the Supreme Court. He stood firm with his nominations, but he also suffered major defeats. He had no difficulty winning confirmation for Warren Burger as chief justice in 1969. But he faced overwhelming opposition the following summer when nominating another strict constructionist for the seat of retiring Justice Fortas. Clement F. Haynsworth, Jr., a Southerner and the chief judge of the Fourth Circuit Court of Appeals, was attacked by civil rights and labor leaders. Their concerns, along with questions about Haynsworth's financial dealings—which dovetailed with the controversy over Fortas's finances and Representative Gerald Ford's drive to impeach Justice William O. Douglas—combined to defeat the nomination.

On poor advice from Mitchell, Nixon then nominated G. Harrold Carswell, who five months earlier had been elevated from a district court to the Fifth Circuit Court of Appeals. Greater furor arose over Carswell's insensitivity to civil rights, and law school deans and professors attacked his mediocre judicial record. In response, Nixon claimed a presidential prerogative to pick whom he wanted; he should have "the same right of choice . . . which has been freely accorded to my predecessors of both parties."[26] That claim was historically inaccurate and unpersuasive. Nixon's second nomination went down by a vote of 45 to 51.

Both the president and the ABA were embarrassed by the rejections. After Carswell's defeat, Nixon took the suggestion of Chief Justice Burger and successfully named fellow Minnesotan Harry Blackmun. The ABA remained under criticism for rating Haynsworth and Carswell, respectively, "highly qualified" and "qualified." Subsequently, because of leaks and unfavorable news stories about possible replacements for retiring Justices John Harlan and Hugo Black, Mitchell refused to provide the ABA with the names of potential nominees. Relations between the ABA and the Justice Department continued to deteriorate in Nixon's final years in office. Nonetheless, the ABA conducted its own investigations of Nixon's last two appointments to the Court: Lewis F. Powell, Jr., a former ABA president, was unanimously endorsed by the ABA; and William Rehnquist, a Nixon administration assistant attorney general, received nine votes in favor of a "highly qualified" ranking and three votes "not opposed" to his appointment.

Nixon failed to bring his legal-policy goals to bear on the selection of lower-court judges. Most often, these judgeships were political rewards, made in deference to senators or in recognition of a nominee's service to the Republican party. As Stephen J. Markman, the assistant attorney general in charge of judicial selection in Reagan's second term, critically observed, "While many Nixon appointees were more conservative judicially than judges selected under earlier administrations, the ability of the Nixon Administration to affect the overall philosophy of the federal bench was ultimately frustrated by the concessions the Administration was forced (or chose) to make."[27]

Ford's Judges

For New Right Republicans in the Reagan administration, the judges picked during Gerald Ford's presidency were a big disappointment. In Markman's words, "the Ford Administration did not make significant changes in the judicial selection process" and "the weakness of the Ford Administration may be seen in the statistic that a record 21 percent of its district court appointments went to members of the opposing party."[28]

But Ford was in a poor position to challenge the norms of judicial selection. He came into the White House as an unelected president, after Nixon resigned, and faced Democratic majorities in Congress. Also, he was a moderate Republican, who did not "view the philosophical grounding of [judicial] candidates to be as important" as did those in the Reagan administration.[29]

Ford was dedicated to restoring the reputation of the presidency, which had suffered a "crisis of confidence," and that of the Justice Department. He perceived the selection of judges as basically a routine staff operation for the Justice Department. Rather than imposing legal-policy goals on judicial selection, the administration sought cooperation from the Senate. Ford picked Edward H. Levi, from the University of Chicago school of law, for attorney general.[30] Levi handled judgeships for a couple of months, but then found that he was too busy with other matters and that most of these matters were routine—"a waste of the attorney general's time."[31] Thereafter, Levi gave the task to deputy attorney general Harold Tyler, a former federal judge, who was assisted by two career attorneys.

Tyler worked to rebuild relations with the ABA and to make sound—not partisan—appointments. He enjoyed a "virtually free hand" and conferred with Levi only after conducting his own investigations of nominees. Except for the appointment of John Paul Stevens to the seat vacated by Justice Douglas in 1975, Levi and Tyler had few dealings with the White House staff on judgeships—though Ford was often at the center of infighting within the White House over the appointment of more conservatives and women.

Carter's Legacy

The election of Jimmy Carter in 1976 brought historic changes to judicial selection and, ultimately, to the federal bench. Carter's primary goal was to make the judiciary more "representative" by appointing women, blacks, and other minorities. As Carter explained, "If I didn't have to get Senate confirmation of appointees, I could tell you flatly that 12 percent of my appointees would be Black and 3 percent would be Spanish-speaking and 40 percent would be women and so forth." His attorney general, Griffin Bell, affirmed that "Carter was prepared to appoint to the federal bench a Black, Hispanic, or woman lawyer who was found to be less qualified than a White male so long as the appointee was found qualified."[32]

As a result, the traditional norms and procedures of judicial selection were challenged and restructured. Senatorial patronage was cut back at the level of appellate court judges. The selection of nominees for the federal bench was "opened up" and decentralized through the use of "merit" or nominating commissions. The names of nominees were given to the National Bar Association and, on a more ad hoc basis, to women's organizations along with the ABA for investigation. Through these commissions, the number of participants in judicial selection grew, but without adding to the Justice Department bureaucracy.

These changes were initiated shortly after the presidential election. Carter and Bell met with Senate Judiciary Committee Chairman Eastland and won support for a plan to create nominating commissions for circuit court judges. When he was governor of Georgia, Carter had used similar commissions to pick state judges. At the federal level, though, his plan expanded presidential power at the expense of senatorial patronage.[33] Carter succeeded where his predecessors failed. In 1977, by executive order, he created a "United States Circuit Court Judge Nomination Commission," with separate panels for each circuit.[34]

Subsequently, Congress passed the Omnibus Judgeship Act of 1978, creating 152 new judgeships and requiring the president to establish a comprehensive plan for selecting judges. Carter issued another executive order on the appointment of district court judges.[35] This order encouraged, but did not compel, senators to set up their own commissions. The attorney general was authorized to review their procedures and to ensure that women and minorities got fair consideration. In addition, general standards were set for candidates' qualifications based on their health, legal experience, community leadership, and "commitment to equal justice under law."

Carter's nominating commissions were widely criticized.[36] They were far from bipartisan—an estimated 85 percent of their members were active Democrats—and they did not eliminate politics or establish "true" merit selection.[37]

Initially, fewer than half of the states (twenty-two) created the district judge nominating commissions, though by 1979 an additional nine states had joined the ranks. In those states that had them, membership, activities, and nominees varied widely. In states with Republican senators, commissions were more bipartisan; in states with Democratic senators, the commissions sometimes exercised considerable independence, sometimes they were simply a facade for nominating the choices of the senators. As a result, numerous confrontations arose over the names submitted by the nominating commissions.

One of the main criticisms was that candidates were asked about their views on controversial issues of legal and social policy. In a major study for the American Judicature Society, based on interviews with candidates and commission members, Larry Berkson and Susan Carbon found that "applicants had often been questioned [by members of the nominating commissions] about nine contemporary social issues [including] the Equal Rights Amendment, affirmative action . . . abortion, capital punishment, busing, economic regulation and a number of Supreme Court cases."[38] Despite the criticism, the questioning of nominees by commissions set a precedent, as did the questions posed to Carter nominees by conservative Senators Strom Thurmond and Orrin Hatch.[39]

Bell, deputy attorney general Michael Egan, and Daniel Meador, the assistant attorney general who drafted the executive order creating the commissions, however, strongly opposed such questioning. In Bell's view, it "politicized the process badly. I don't believe that you should ask a judge his views [on specific issues] because he is likely to have to rule on that."[40]

Bell, a former federal judge and a conservative Democrat, assumed leadership within the Justice Department. Unlike prior attorneys general, he did not delegate responsibility, though he relied on Egan and career attorney Phil Modlin (both registered Republicans) to handle initial recommendations coming from the commissions, senators, and others. Bell read each candidate's file and reports from the FBI and the ABA. He also gave the National Bar Association the opportunity to respond to potential nominees. He further required an Internal Revenue Service investigation of candidates' financial affairs and a medical examination. He did not, however, meet with candidates except to discuss concerns raised by the ABA or others. Bell stopped the FBI from reporting on the political affiliation of candidates, stating that "I have no interest in what party they are in as long as they are good people." Of course, Bell could identify the party faithful from their files. Still, he opposed looking at ideological orientation and packing the bench with women, blacks, or other minorities. In this, he sometimes had to combat White House staff seeking to influence the selection of judges.[41]

Thus, without scrutinizing nominees' judicial philosophy or seeking to impose its own political view on the federal bench, the Carter administration pushed affirmative action goals. As Egan explained, "we never talked about whether this guy would support the policies of the president; there was no going into ideological or thought processes."[42] Still, like all administrations, Carter favored the party faithful.

Reagan's Judges

President Reagan's judicial selection reflects his administration's goal of appointing conservatives and advocates of judicial restraint. In a 1986 speech, Reagan assessed his administration's efforts to remake the federal bench: "I am pleased to be able to tell you that I've already appointed 284 federal judges, men and women who share the fundamental values that you and I so cherish, and that by the time we leave office, our administration will have appointed some 45 percent of all federal judges."[43] Those in the administration say that they are exercising the president's prerogative to restore political balance to the judiciary and ensure the "Reagan legacy."[44]

Whether the politics of judgeships in the Reagan era differs in kind—or only in degree—from that of previous administrations is a matter of debate. Indisputably, the administration has a more coherent and ambitious legal-policy agenda that has been more systematically, meticulously, and effectively imposed than that of any prior administration. "The Reagan administration," according to Stephen Markman, the assistant attorney general in charge of judicial selection in Reagan's second term, "has in place what is probably the most thorough and comprehensive system for recruiting and screening federal judicial candidates of any administration ever. This Administration has, moreover, attempted to assert the President's prerogatives over judicial selection more consistently than many of its predecessors."[45]

From the outset, according to Bruce Fein, a former associate deputy attorney general who helped to set up the judicial selection operation, greater control was necessary if the administration was to reverse past trends that were pushing toward the selection of moderate to liberal judges.[46] One of the first steps was to eliminate Carter's nominating commissions, and Reagan also requested senators to submit three to five names for each district court vacancy.[47]

Presidential control was furthered by abandoning Carter's policy of working with the National Bar Association—representing black lawyers—and women's organizations. Under attorneys general William French Smith and Edwin Meese, these groups no longer participated in judicial selection. The relationship with the ABA changed too, particularly after some of Reagan's nominees ran into trouble. The attitude toward the ABA within the Justice Department was at times hostile; in Fein's words, "we didn't think one second about ABA ratings."[48]

Within the Justice Department, judicial selection was reorganized and subject to greater White House supervision. The attorney general no longer assumed total responsibility. A White House Judicial Selection Committee—which includes the attorney general; the deputy attorney general; the counselor to the president; assistant attorneys general for the Office of Legal Policy, Personnel and Legislation; and White House advisers (among them the chief of staff)—was created to decide whom the president should nominate. This reorganization concentrated power within—and institutionalized the role of—the White House and better positioned the administration to combat senatorial patronage.

In addition, a rigorous screening process was introduced. First, candidates' records are scrutinized and compared with those of others, using computer data banks that contain published speeches, articles, and opinions of hundreds of potential nominees. Then, candidates undergo several daylong interviews with Justice Department officials. Markman estimates that in the process of selecting some 300 judges, "over 1,000 individuals have been interviewed."[49] According to Sheldon Goldman, the interviews enabled "consistent ideological or policy orientation screening."[50] Fred Fielding, former counselor to the president, agreed that the administration's process is designed to choose "people of a certain judicial philosophy."[51]

Fein and the administration defended the interviews on the ground that "a president who fails to scrutinize the legal philosophy of federal judicial nominees courts frustration of his own policy agenda." They criticized past Republican administrations for failing to take seriously judicial philosophy and simply looking to "a candidate's reputation and standing."[52]

But the questions asked at these interviews have stirred considerable controversy. Some who made it to the bench and others who didn't say they were asked for their views on abortion, affirmative action, and criminal justice. Nina Totenberg of National Public Radio cites one female state court judge as stating, "I guess most of us have accepted that we're not going to get these judgeships unless we're willing to commit to a particular position which we think would be improper."[53]

This kind of ideological screening draws criticism not only from liberal senators and organizations but also from those who were in past Republican administrations and conservative law professors. University of Chicago law school professor Philip Kurland, for one, charges that "judges are being appointed in the expectation that they will rewrite laws and the Constitution to the administration's liking. Reagan's judges are activists in support of conservative dogma—what some people would call hanging judges in criminal law and anti-regulation judges in civil law."[54]

Philip Lacovara, a Republican and former official in Nixon's Justice Department, resigned as Reagan's representative on the nominating commission for the District of Columbia courts because he was viewed as not conservative enough for consideration for a judgeship. According to Lacovara, officials told him that he was "too liberal," "not politically reliable," and that he had failed the "litmus test for philosophical orthodoxy." He claims that "ideology is the primary qualification, and it is a candidate's demonstrated orthodoxy that brings his name before the President and ultimately before the Senate. Unique in our nation's history, the current Justice Department has been processing any judicial candidate through a series of officials whose primary duty is to assess the candidate's ideological purity."[55]

The Reagan administration denies that it has a "litmus test." As Fielding puts it, there is "no one factor" considered.[56] The administration claims that candidates are asked about past rulings and hypothetical cases—dealing, admittedly, with controversial issues like abortion—in order to "see how they think through a case" and where they stand on the role of courts. According to Meese, "we do discuss the law with judicial candidates. . . . In discussing the law with lawyers there is really no way not to bring up cases—past cases—and engage in a dialogue over the reasoning and merits of particular decisions. But even here, our primary interest is how someone's mind works, whether they have powers of discernment and the scholarly grounding required of a good judge."[57]

But such explanations satisfy few critics—particularly moderate Republican senators whose nominees for the federal bench have been opposed by Justice Department officials and "New Right" senators such as Orrin Hatch, Jeremiah Denton, and the late John P. East. The refusal of the administration to bargain or bend on its own legal-policy goals thus has lead to delays in filling judgeships and to intraparty conflict. In Pennsylvania, for example, six vacancies remain open after almost two years. One candidate, James R. McGregor, a respected trial court judge who has the support of Pennsylvania's two Republican senators (Arlen Specter and John Heinz), was not nominated by the Justice Department for two years because it viewed him as too lenient on criminal justice matters; but, after the Democrats regained the Senate in 1986, it finally agreed to his nomination.[58]

Judith Whittaker and Andrew L. Frey are two respected attorneys who were turned down. The Justice Department refused to nominate Whittaker, associate general counsel of Hallmark Cards and highly rated by the ABA, because she supported the Equal Rights Amendment and was viewed as antibusiness and proabortion. Frey, who was deputy solicitor general within the Justice Department, had made donations to Planned Parenthood and the National Coalition to Ban Handguns. This information was revealed when Senators East and Denton requested that Frey fill out a questionnaire (reprinted in Appendix A) asking his views on abortion, religion, school desegregation, and affirmative action. Subsequently, along with Hatch and ten other senators, they prevailed upon the administration not to nominate him.

The administration's hard-line position with moderate Republican senators has led to some tough battles and some defeats. The nomination of Jefferson B. Sessions III to a district court in Alabama was narrowly defeated within the Senate Judiciary Committee in 1986; this happened only once before in the past forty-eight years.[59] Sherman E. Unger, the only Reagan nominee thus far rated "not qualified" by the ABA, faced stiff opposition; he died before his confirmation.[60] Several others—such as Sidney Fitzwater, Alex Kozinski, and former Senator

James Buckley—also ran into trouble.[61] And Reagan was forced to withdraw the nominations of law school professors William Harvey and Lino Graglia due to unfavorable ABA reports and strong political opposition.[62]

Nonetheless, the Reagan administration has had a major influence on the composition, and perhaps the future direction, of the judiciary.[63] It has named few women, blacks, or other minorities, concentrating instead on younger, upper-middle-class white males.[64] In Fielding's words, younger judges with a track record of aggressive conservatism are "Ronald Reagan's best legacy."

Conclusion

The selection of federal judges has always been political. Traditionally, presidents rewarded party faithful and accommodated senatorial patronage. But recent presidents—particularly Carter and Reagan—have tried to remold the judiciary in light of their own legal-policy goals. Carter sought to open up the selection process and bring diversity to the federal bench; Reagan has sought to appoint only judicial conservatives.

Liberals and conservatives in both political parties object to the renewed assertion of presidential power over lower-court judgeships and to the rigorous screening process put into place by the Reagan administration. Yet, there is no gainsaying that presidents have the constitutional authority to do as they please when nominating federal judges. At the same time, the Senate's role in scrutinizing and confirming judges becomes more critical and controversial.

· 4 ·

Senate Confirmation: A Rubber Stamp?

A LTHOUGH THE SENATE has the power to reject nominees to the federal bench put forward by the president, the overwhelming majority of nominees are routinely approved by the Senate Judiciary Committee and confirmed by the Senate after only perfunctory investigation and according to no fixed standards. As Philip Kurland commented, "the Senate as a whole ordinarily acknowledges [senatorial courtesy] by paying less attention to the confirmation process of a federal judge than to the price of bean soup in the Senate restaurants."[1] According to a Senate Judiciary Committee staffer, the Senate as a whole rarely considers the qualifications of nominees, and the investigation of their backgrounds by the committee is "as *pro forma* as *pro forma* can be."[2] Senators in both parties agree that the increasing number of judgeships makes such routine processing—or "rubber-stamping"—of nominees inappropriate.[3]

If the Senate is to play a more active role in judicial selection, then clear standards must be established for confirming or rejecting nominees. At present, according to a recent study for Common Cause by Michal Freedman, the Senate Judicial Committee "has no affirmative standards for confirmation. It seems willing to endorse a nominee unless charges of criminal or flagrantly unethical behavior are proved."[4]

What "standard" should apply in rejecting judicial nominees remains sharply disputed. Theodore Roosevelt, for one, granted the Senate wide latitude. In a letter to a senator whose candidate he declined to nominate, he put it this way:

> It is, I trust, needless to say that I fully appreciate the right and duty of the Senate to reject or to confirm any appointment according to what its members conscientiously deem their duty to be; just as it is my business to make an appointment which I conscientiously think is a good one.[5]

Richard Nixon, on the other hand, maintained during G. Harrold Carswell's nomination that:

> What is centrally at issue . . . is the constitutional responsibility of the president to appoint members of the Court—and whether this responsibility can be frustrated by those who wish to substitute their own philosophy or their own subjective judgment for that of the one person entrusted by the Constitution with the power of appointment.[6]

The debate turns on whether it is appropriate for the Senate to consider the nominee's ideological orientation. New Right Republican senators—like Hatch, Denton, East, and Jesse Helms—press the view that the nominee's ideological outlook is fair game. Democratic senators—like Simon, Leahy, and Joseph Biden—have argued that it is inappropriate; they have failed, however, to come up with specific nonpartisan or nonideological standards for confirming or rejecting nominees. It also remains debatable whether such standards, as urged by Kurland and Harvard Law School professor Laurence Tribe, are possible and whether bipartisan agreement would be feasible.[7]

The Senate's "Advice and Consent"

Although the Senate has the power to reject the president's nominees for the Supreme Court, it is a power that is rarely exercised. Altogether, only twelve nominees have been rejected by the Senate. An additional sixteen nominees were withdrawn from consideration, or their nominations were indefinitely postponed because of senate opposition.[8] Table 4.1 shows Supreme Court nominations rejected, postponed, or withdrawn because of Senate opposition.

There is even less controversy over the appointment of lower federal court judges. Most are routinely approved by the Senate Judiciary Committee and are confirmed by the full Senate without debate or roll-call votes.

In a study of judicial confirmations between 1951 and 1962, Joel Grossman found that the Senate Judiciary Committee recommended 98 percent (or 301 out of 307) of the nominations received. In most cases, there was no independent investigation, and the committee recommended Senate confirmation less than two weeks after what can be described only as perfunctory hearings. Grossman concluded that "the Senate Judiciary Committee's major function in the selection process is to rein-

Table 4.1
Supreme Court Nominations Rejected, Postponed, or Withdrawn due to Senate Opposition

Nominee	Year Nominated	Nominated By	Actions[1]
William Paterson[2]	1793	Washington	Withdrawn (for technical reasons)
John Rutledge[3]	1795	Washington	Rejected
Alexander Wolcott	1811	Madison	Rejected
John J. Crittenden	1828	J. Q. Adams	Postponed, 1829
Roger B. Taney[4]	1835	Jackson	Postponed
John C. Spencer	1844	Tyler	Rejected
Reuben H. Walworth	1844	Tyler	Withdrawn
Edward King	1844	Tyler	Postponed
Edward King[5]	1844	Tyler	Withdrawn, 1845
John M. Read	1845	Tyler	No action
George W. Woodward	1845	Polk	Rejected, 1846
Edward A. Bradford	1852	Fillmore	No action
George E. Badger	1853	Fillmore	Postponed
William C. Micou	1853	Fillmore	No action
Jeremiah S. Black	1861	Buchanan	Rejected
Henry Stanbery	1866	Johnson	No action
Ebenezer R. Hoar	1869	Grant	Rejected, 1870
George H. Williams[3]	1873	Grant	Withdrawn, 1874
Caleb Cushing[3]	1874	Grant	Withdrawn
Stanley Matthews[2]	1881	Hayes	No action
William B. Hornblower	1893	Cleveland	Rejected, 1894
Wheeler H. Peckham	1894	Cleveland	Rejected
John J. Parker	1930	Hoover	Rejected
Abe Fortas[6]	1968	Johnson	Withdrawn
Homer Thornberry	1968	Johnson	No action
Clement F. Haynsworth, Jr.	1969	Nixon	Rejected
G. Harrold Carswell	1970	Nixon	Rejected
Robert H. Bork	1987	Reagan	Rejected
Douglas H. Ginsburg	1987	Reagan	Withdrawn

[1]A year is given if different from the year of nomination. [2]Reappointed and confirmed. [3]Nominated for chief justice. [4]Taney was reappointed and confirmed as chief justice. [5]Second appointment. [6]Associate justice nominated for chief justice.
Source: Library of Congress, Congressional Research Service.

force and protect the prerogative of individual senators to control lower judicial nominations in their states or, alternatively, to insure that presidential nominations do not violate any of the rules of the game."[9]

Little has changed in the past twenty-five years. Except during Edward Kennedy's chairmanship of the Senate Judiciary Committee, most nominees have been expeditiously approved, with little or no independent inquiry and only brief hearings before a subcommittee composed of one or two senators. (See Table 4.2.)

The processing of nominees during the 99th Congress (1985-86) is illustrative. The Senate Judiciary Committee considered 136 nominees; only 6 were given more than one pro forma hearing. Only one nominee—Jefferson B. Sessions III for district court judge—failed to obtain committee approval. Of those nominees who faced more than one hearing, two—Stanley Sporkin and George Revercomb—were later confirmed as district judges (without a record vote) by the full Senate. The four others—

Table 4.2

Nominations before the Senate Judiciary Committee (1965-86)
Average Number of Days
between Nominees' Referral and Hearings

Chairman	Congress	Appellate Court Judges	District Court Judges
Eastland	89th	17.1	19.5
	90th	22.0	29.8
	91st	19.8	27.8
	92nd	24.7	18.9
	93rd	17.4	20.5
	94th	22.0	30.3
	95th	20.2	23.2
Kennedy	96th	66.2	55.5
Thurmond	97th	23.8	20.7
	98th	15.2	16.7
	99th	22.5	23.2

Source: Based on data supplied by the Senate Judiciary Committee.

Alex Kozinski and Daniel Manion for appellate court judges, and Sessions and Sidney Fitzwater for district court judges—became the subjects of heated confirmation battles.

The Senate, however, failed to reject a single lower-court nominee. Besides Kozinski, Manion, and Fitzwater, it had roll-call votes on only three others—Chief Justice William Rehnquist, Justice Antonin Scalia, and former Senator James Buckley for the Court of Appeals for the District of Columbia Circuit. In only two cases—Manion and Rehnquist —did the Senate Judiciary Committee bother to file reports on the nominees with the full Senate. For most, not even a transcript of their hearings was available before the vote.

The Judiciary Committee's rubber-stamping of nominees has not escaped criticism on the Senate floor. Senator Carl Levin, who led the fight against Kozinski, did so on evidence that he claimed was not fully considered by the committee—that is, Kozinski's temperament and allegations that he had humiliated subordinates, mishandled cases, and misrepresented his record as special counsel for the Merit Systems Protection Board.[10] Kozinski won Senate approval, but only by a vote of 54 to 43. In another instance, although five members of the Judiciary Committee voted against Fitzwater, the Senate was not given a report on his qualifications or on allegations that he was insensitive toward black voting rights. During the floor debate, Senator Paul Sarbanes voiced his dissatisfaction with the lack of communication:

> Far be it from me really to intrude into the procedures of the Judiciary Committee, but it does seem to me that if we are going to have controversial nominations on the floor of the Senate—and this obviously is such a nomination, with a fairly close cloture vote, and I assume a fairly close vote on confirmation—we ought to have a report, or at a minimum that the hearings of the Committee should be printed so that the Members of the Senate can have the opportunity to at least have the printed hearing record before them and be in a position to review it.[11]

Fitzwater was confirmed by a vote of 52 to 42.

There are few incentives for the Senate to do other than approve the vast majority of lower federal court nominees. It costs senators to battle with their colleagues over these nominees and gains them little with their constituents; the lack of agreement on standards for confirming nominees also contributes, and few interest groups have pushed for more rigor.

Senatorial Courtesy

Senatorial courtesy—that is, respect for individual senator's preferences and patronage in filling vacancies—has a negative impact on judicial selection in that it protects the patronage of individual senators. But it also has a positive impact, as it safeguards senators' influence on nominations.

Historically, senators took the lead in recommending candidates to the Justice Department for the lower federal courts in their home states; only one candidate's name would be submitted per vacancy. (Presidents traditionally had wider discretion in nominating judges for appellate courts and the Supreme Court.) Should the candidate be a Senate member or former member, the Senate usually extends courtesy by immediately confirming the nominee.

The traditional practice of senators submitting only one name for each vacancy led to some very poor appointments. As former attorney general Elliot Richardson complained, it "diminish[es] the quality of the federal judiciary by unduly restricting the pool of potential nominees."[12] Both Carter and Reagan requested three to five recommendations for each vacancy, but some senators have refused to give up their patronage. As the former Judiciary Committee chairman James Eastland told Griffin Bell, when refusing to give him more than one name for each vacancy, "I'll hand you a slip of paper with one name on it, and that'll be the judge."[13] More senators, though, send three to five names to the Justice Department for each vacancy, often suggesting their preference. Some senators now rely on nominating commissions. And some—such as New York senators Alfonse D'Amato, a Republican, and Daniel Moynihan, a Democrat—rotate choices on vacancies, conferring with a state judicial selection committee.

The Blue-Slip Rejection

Last century, all that was necessary for a home-state senator to veto a nominee was to announce on the Senate floor that the nominee was "personally obnoxious." By the mid-1940s, though, there was an expectation that the senator explain his opposition. The home-state senator's power to veto virtually any nominee from his state was institutionalized in the form of a "blue slip"—literally a blue piece of paper sent by the Judiciary Committee to the home-state senator that read:

Dear Senator:

Will you kindly give me, for the use of the Committee, your opinion and information concerning the nomination of [name, district, and name of former judge]. Under rule of the Committee, unless a reply is received from you within a week from this date, it will be assumed that you have no objection to this nomination.

Respectfully,
[Signature]
Chairman, Senate Judiciary Committee

Although the wording would seem to indicate that nonreturn signifies support for the nominee, in practice it meant exactly the opposite. If the senator did not return the blue slip, it was determined that he opposed the nomination. As a result, the committee would not recommend the nominee and the senator would not have to oppose the nomination on the Senate floor.

For twenty-five years, the blue slip stood as a virtually insurmountable barrier for nominees opposed by home-state senators.[14] As Nixon's attorney general, John Mitchell, said, "Those blue slips are the tickets to the ballgame."[15] This practice changed when Edward Kennedy chaired the Judiciary Committee. At the outset, he announced that failure to return a blue slip would not bar the committee from holding hearings nor from sending a nomination on for Senate confirmation. Although a confrontation never arose during Kennedy's chairmanship (1979-81), not returning the blue slip is no longer a hard-and-fast veto.

When Senator Strom Thurmond assumed chairmanship in 1981, he enforced Kennedy's policy. In addition, he requested that senators state, if they so believe, that a nominee is "personally obnoxious" when they respond to the blue slip. Thus, even when Senator William Proxmire opposed a candidate from his home state, Thurmond nevertheless held hearings and, during them, established that Proxmire did not find the nominee "personally obnoxious."[16] When home-state Senator Daniel Inouye raised objections to another Reagan nominee, Albert Moon, Thurmond held hearings but failed to report this nomination out of committee to the full Senate.[17]

The blue slip is now rarely used to block nominees. But in a 1980 survey of senators and staff, Elliot Slotnick found that senators considered it a valuable tool for enhancing their negotiating position with the administration.[18] Their success with that tool, however, still depends on their own prestige, the prevailing view of the Senate toward the administration, and the policies of the chairman of the Senate Judiciary Committee.

The Senate Judiciary Committee

The chairman of the Senate Judiciary Committee is in an especially powerful position when it comes to judicial selection. How he runs the committee determines when a president's nominees have hearings and usually whether and how much opposition they encounter. By delaying Senate action on confirmation, the chairman may pressure the president or test his support for nominees, as well as allow fellow senators to gather support or opposition. Hearings also may be used to embarrass a nominee or the president and, of course, to create a record that recommends against confirmation.

Despite criticism of the committee's rubber-stamping of most nominees, the trend in the past forty years has been toward greater scrutiny of nominees. Prior to 1947, public hearings were held only for controversial nominees, and often these hearings were neither transcribed nor printed. Richard Burke reports that between 1920 and 1955, fewer than thirty hearings on judicial nominees were held and printed.[19] Hearings—although superficial—are now held on all nominees and later published. In addition, since the 1940s, the chairman of the Judiciary Committee (or his designate) receives a copy of the confidential FBI reports made on the nominees for the Justice Department. The chairman also now receives copies of the rating given the nominee by the ABA and a questionnaire (reprinted in Appendix B) filled out by the nominee.

The approach of the chairman of the Judiciary Committee toward judicial nominees determines, to a large extent, whether the Senate exercises its check on the president's choices for the federal bench.

Mississippi's conservative Democratic Senator James Eastland, who headed the committee from 1956 to 1979, maintained almost total control over appointments. For instance, he delayed the confirmation of blacks by Democratic administrations for months. John Holloman, a former committee staff director, recalled that during Republican administrations, "the judges they pick for Mississippi might be Republicans but they are Eastland Republicans."[20]

Eastland had no special staff to investigate nominees; he relied instead on one of his aides. Except for nominations to the Supreme Court, he did not utilize the full Judiciary Committee to consider nominees.

Instead, he appointed an ad hoc subcommittee to consider all lower-court nominees. The subcommittee consisted of Eastland, John McClellan (the ranking Democrat on the Judiciary Committee), and Roman Hruska (the ranking Republican)—three of the committee's most conservative members. Like hearings for the vast majority of nominees held under other chairmen, Eastland's were brief and superficial.

When Edward Kennedy assumed chairmanship, he forged major changes.[21] Besides changing the ground rules for blue slips, Kennedy pushed for independent investigations of nominees. A Judiciary Committee questionnaire was developed and sent to nominees along with those of the ABA and the Justice Department. Notices of hearings were sent to the press and put in the *Congressional Record;* interest groups were invited to give their views on nominees.[22] For the first time, the Judiciary Committee also had its own special investigative staff to review the qualifications of nominees. The staff consisted of one full-time and one part-time investigator, an FBI agent to help on "hard cases," a paralegal, and a secretary.[23] Thomas Sussman, who served as general counsel for the Judiciary Committee under Kennedy, recalls that the staff was small in comparison to those of other congressional committees, but that it conducted more thorough investigations. The National Bar Association, the NAACP Legal Defense Fund, and a range of women's organizations also brought concerns to light and helped track down information on nominees. Elaine Jones, who reviews nominations for the NBA and the NAACP Legal Defense Fund, however, points out that these organizations rely on "grass-roots" members, and the flow of information is inevitably uneven and ad hoc.[24]

The Judiciary Committee shifted direction again when Strom Thurmond became chairman in 1981. For one thing, although the number of judgeships annually granted was steadily increasing, the size of the investigative staff was reduced. In addition, Thurmond and his principal investigator, Duke Short, were less open to the concerns of outside groups—especially liberal civil rights organizations—and their own investigation of nominees slipped.

During his six years as chairman (1981-86), Thurmond proved an influential ally of the Reagan administration. In the words of one committee staffer, Thurmond was "willing to swallow and push the most controversial of Reagan's nominees."[25] The unsuccessful Sessions nomination illustrates the extent to which the Reagan administration and Thurmond cooperated.

The administration, the ABA, and Thurmond knew that Sessions's nomination to a district court in Alabama would meet severe opposition. As a U.S. attorney, Sessions had described the NAACP and the American Civil Liberties Union as "un-American," had made racially insensitive remarks, and had unsuccessfully prosecuted black leaders for ballot-tampering. A number of attorneys described him as "petty, vindictive and not having the proper temperament to serve as a federal judge."[26] During his hearing before the Judiciary Committee, Sessions angered senators by changing positions—claiming that his earlier statements had been taken out of context. In the end, a bipartisan group within the committee turned against Thurmond and voted 10 to 8 to reject Sessions and on a 9 to 9 tie vote thwarted the committee's sending his name on to the full Senate for confirmation. The most dramatic moment was when home-state Senator Howell Heflin cast a negative vote: "My conscience is not clear and I must vote no," he said, emphasizing that he was troubled by "the alleged inconsistencies" in Sessions's testimony. "There are admissions, explanations, partial admissions, statements about jokes," Heflin, a former judge, explained, concluding, "a person should not be confirmed for a lifetime appointment as a district judge if there are reasonable doubts about his ability to be fair and impartial."[27]

Thurmond's use of his position to push Reagan's nominees led to increasing battles within the Judiciary Committee. The struggle initially emerged because Thurmond gave in to pressures from New Right members of the committee who opposed nominees they considered too moderate on such issues as abortion and gun control. New Right Senators Jeremiah Denton, John East, and Orrin Hatch took the unprecedented step of sending nominees their own questionnaires seeking nominees' views of Supreme Court rulings on abortion, the death penalty, the exclusionary role—barring the use at trial of illegally obtained evidence—affirmative action, and freedom of religion. (The questionnaire sent to Andrew Frey and Joseph Rodriguez is reprinted in Appendix A.) By asking questions about specific rulings, Denton, East, and Hatch broke with tradition and implicitly challenged Thurmond's position as chairman. Ultimately, Democratic senators forced Thurmond to get Denton, East, and Hatch to stop sending out the questionnaire. The dispute, however, polarized Thurmond's committee.

And that was not the only source of conflict. Thurmond pushed through the committee a larger number of nominees in a shorter period of time than had Kennedy as chairman. Under Kennedy, the average time between a nomination and hearings was two months. Under Thurmond, that dropped to twenty days, and then committee votes on nominees usually were scheduled for just ten days later—twice as fast as under Kennedy. Senator Paul Simon complained that "We have not given close enough scrutiny to these nominees. . . . We have so many names coming at us so rapidly it becomes difficult for us to do the kind of intensive work that needs to be done."[28]

Democrats on the Judiciary Committee had only two staff people who divided their time between reviewing nominees and other work. Reggie Govan, an aide to the ranking Democrat, Joseph Biden, estimated that he "spent 75 to 95 percent of his time on judicial appointments but . . . just the controversial ones." The Democrats relied heavily on interest groups to monitor local newspapers and to alert them about controversial nominees. According to Govan, they were "to be an early warning system but it never really materialized—never became an effective warning system."[29] But as Nan Aron, the director of the Alliance for Justice, points out, the Republicans had a tactical advantage. "When you speed [nominations] through, you preclude outside groups and senators' staffs from taking a good hard look at these candidates."[30]

In late 1985, Thurmond and ranking Democrats on the committee reached agreement to wait at least three weeks between a nomination and holding hearings and to allow as long as two weeks more before voting on nominees. This agreement also placed a limit on the number of nominees who could be considered at any point to six, and permitted unlimited time for considering the nominees whom the Democrats singled out as controversial. In addition, the committee's questionnaire was revised. First, it was (once again) to provide for the release of financial disclosure statements by nominees. (These had been available until 1984, when Thurmond bowed to Justice Department pressure for the withholding of such information.) Further, additional questions about the nominees' legal practices were to be included.

With the 1986 congressional elections, Democrats regained the Senate, and Biden took over the chairmanship of the Judiciary Committee. By Senate agreement on committee assignments, the committee shrank from eighteen to fourteen members, eliminating three conservative Republican activists—most notably North Carolina's Senator Jesse Helms. In addition, Biden created a four-member panel—headed by Senator Leahy—to screen nominees; the panel is assisted by three staff investigators.

Whether the Biden committee will restore independent investigation and toughen the committee's standards remains uncertain. Leahy has emphasized that "the phrase 'routine judicial nominations' will be banished from the committee's vocabulary" and that it will "open up the process . . . make a record on every nominee that comes before it [and] consider the standards for judicial nominees."[31] And during the first six months of 1987, the 1st Session of the 100th Congress, the administration was slow to fill vacancies and named few controversial conservatives.

Whose and What Standards?

Neither the Constitution nor political practice provides precise guidelines for judicial selection. As a result, the vast majority of nominees are routinely confirmed according to no fixed standards.

The Senate's standards are basically parochial—based on each senator's personal views and partisanship. Senator Leahy points out, "Of course, there are qualities we would all consider indispensable for a judge: experience, intellectual capacity, temperament, integrity, and a demonstrated commitment to equal justice. We need guidelines for measuring these. A simple checklist won't do. The individual nominees are too diverse to fit a rigid mold. Any rule we lay down may be subject to exceptions."[32] Yet exceptions are the rule, and qualities like "temperament" remain minimal, vague, and unevenly applied criteria. More precise standards are unlikely. Even fairly objective standards such as the ABA's suggestion of a minimal number of years of legal experience are not hard-and-fast.

When controversial nominations are made, the question that usually dominates debate is not what standards should apply, but what the proper role of the Senate should be in scrutinizing the nominees' legal and political views. That the Senate may actively review nominees and even reject them for purely political reasons is clear from the constitutional debates over, and the political history of, the appointment power. From the time of the Senate's defeat of George Washington's proposed elevation of Justice John Rutledge to chief justice in 1795, partisan politics has been considered a fair basis for rejecting nominees—whether because of their party affiliation or views on specific issues.[33] Since 1925, when Harlan F. Stone agreed to appear before the Senate Judiciary Committee, Supreme Court nominees have been asked about their basic judicial philosophies.[34]

In this century, five nominees to the Supreme Court were defeated, and several others—including Harlan Stone, Louis Brandeis, Charles Evans Hughes, and Thurgood Marshall—faced stiff opposition because of their views on socioeconomic and legal policy. John J. Parker, a respected appellate judge, was defeated in 1930 because he was viewed as antiunion and opposed to black voting rights. Opposition in 1968 to Johnson's proposed elevation of Justice Abe Fortas to chief justice centered on Fortas's support for the Warren Court's "liberal jurisprudence." When the Senate defeated Nixon's nominations of Haynsworth and Carswell in 1970, their views on labor law and race relations came under attack. And, as discussed in the epilogue, the bitter confirmation battle over Reagan's nomination of Judge Robert H. Bork resulted in his defeat in 1987.

Thus, when either the Judiciary Committee or the entire Senate confronts controversial nominees, it does so neither as a court applying fixed standards nor as a deliberative council advising the president; it functions like an investigatory committee probing nominees' views.

There are those who contend that the Senate should not ask nominees about their views on specific issues or reject them on that basis either. This view was recently put forth by the Reagan administration when fighting to win the confirmation of Chief Justice Rehnquist.[35] It appears disingenuous, however, for those in the Reagan administration to put forward this argument. More than any other administration, it has sought to achieve its own legal-policy goals through judicial appointments. Also, its New Right supporters in the Senate have subjected nominees to detailed questioning.

Judge Robert Bork once lamented, before his own unsuccessful Supreme Court nomination, the focus on the legal-policy views of nominees, stating that

> It's unfortunate if the selection process focuses in that much detail on specific cases or issues, for two reasons. One is that you don't want to turn the process of becoming a judge into a campaign in which you make campaign promises about what you will do. It should not be a political position. And . . . you may choose a judge for his views on a particular issue, and five years hence that issue will be unimportant and there will be a whole new range of issues that nobody anticipated would become important. . . . For that reason I think it's more important, when you are considering someone to become a judge, to focus upon that person's

approach to legal philosophy and general approach to legal questions, rather than upon the outcome of the particular cases.[36]

Regardless of these objections, however, hearings on controversial nominations have tended to come down to nominees' legal-policy views. After all, if presidents seek nominees because of their legal-policy positions, it is only fitting that senators focus more on these considerations as well. Since judges have the power to interpret the law, senators no less than the president should scrutinize their judicial and political philosophy. Felix Frankfurter, before going to the Court, defended such scrutiny on the ground that, "the meaning of 'due process' and the content of terms like 'liberty' are not revealed by the Constitution. It is the Justices who make the meaning. They read into the neutral language of the Constitution their own economic and social views. . . . Let us face the fact that five justices of the Supreme Court *are* the molders of policy, rather than the impersonal vehicles of revealed truth."[37]

As the judiciary has assumed a larger role in fashioning national public law and policy, the socioeconomic and legal views of nominees have become a more open basis for opposition. When Thurmond attacked Fortas's nomination, for example, he proclaimed that "the Supreme Court has assumed such a powerful role as a policymaker in the government that the Senate must necessarily be concerned with the views of prospective Justices or Chief Justices as they relate to broad issues confronting the American people, and the role of the Court in dealing with these issues."[38] Similarly, when West Virginia's conservative Democratic Senator Robert Byrd voted against Justice Thurgood Marshall's confirmation, he stated, "I simply cannot bring myself to vote for an individual to be a United States Supreme Court Justice who, by his past record so clearly stamps himself as one who will be an ally to the already top-heavy, ultraliberal and activist bloc on the Court."[39]

Less than five years later, liberal Democratic Senators Kennedy, Birch Bayh, Philip Bart, and John Tunney opposed Justice Rehnquist's confirmation. They claimed his "views on the large issues of the day will make it harmful to the country for him to sit and vote the Court."[40] In 1986, when Kennedy opposed Rehnquist's elevation to the center chair on the high court, he maintained that he "was too extreme to be Chief Justice. . . . He is wrong on equal rights for women, wrong on separation of church and state, wrong on basic individual freedoms in the First Amendment."[41] And in 1987 it was Bork's judicial philosophy that doomed his confirmation.

Some senators and scholars worry, in attorney Lew Paper's words, that "uninhibited review of a nominee's philosophy could lead to protracted battles between the President and the Senate that would boil down to a single contest of which institution exercised the greater influence" and that in the process the stature of the judiciary will suffer.[42] But there is no constitutional prohibition on uninhibited review and every reason for it—especially since presidents now try to refashion the judiciary as a means of achieving their own legal-policy goals. As law professor Donald Lively points out,

> A constitutional system based upon separation of powers presupposes that no single branch is to be pervasively dominant. The principle is endangered, however, if the President endeavors to shape the Judiciary and the Senate merely defers to the Executive. Although the Senate may afford the President ample latitude in purely Executive appointments, because such persons are hired to work for the Executive, just the opposite is true of the Judiciary. Judges do not serve the President but are supposed to be independent of and a check upon the Executive.[43]

Chief Justice Rehnquist has long supported senatorial scrutiny of "the views of a new Justice on constitution interpretation."[44] Though during his own confirmation hearings he maintained that judges should not answer questions about specific cases, in 1957 he attacked the "startling dearth of inquiry" preceding Justice Charles Whittaker's confirmation. Later, during the Fortas controversy, he ridiculed the logic of those who insisted on senatorial restraint. They, he observed, "are reduced to contending . . . that even though the President . . . can and does consider the judicial philosophy of the appointee, the Senate when it debates confirmation may not consider it."[45]

Moderate senators and scholars have urged the establishment of guidelines for modest—yet thorough—scrutiny of nominees.[46] Conservative law professor Philip Kurland and liberal Harvard Law School professor Laurence Tribe came together to urge the Judiciary Committee to adopt higher standards for confirming nominees. But in Kurland and Tribe's proposal, the standards, subject to personal interpretation, would fail to command agreement. For example, Tribe argues that senators should vote against nominees if their philosophy is inconsistent with "the American vision of a just society" or if the appointee would "upset the Court's equilibrium or exacerbate what [the senator] views as an already excessive conservative or liberal bias."[47] Yet, such "standards" lack precision, guidance, and predictability. And they are the very grounds on which senators most often disagree.

Conclusion

The Senate's standards are likely to remain parochial. Its routine operating procedures preserve patronage and provide no incentives for reaching higher standards. For that reason reformers are bound to meet little success. More feasible and likely to improve the quality of appointees are procedural changes along the lines of those made during Kennedy's chairmanship of the Judiciary Committee.[48] More investigative staff needs to review the qualifications of nominees—particularly now that the Senate must pass on fifty or more judgeships annually. There should be adequate public notice of the nominees being considered and at least a month between nominations and hearings. Interest groups that monitor judicial appointments should be assured opportunities to provide information to the Judiciary Committee. Such measures, rather than a search for alluring but nevertheless elusive precision in standards, would make the confirmation process more rigorous and the politics of appointing judges more open and accountable.

· 5 ·

The Role of the
American Bar Association

HAS THE American Bar Association's involvement in judicial appointments improved the quality of the federal bench, or has it done little more than help eliminate a few of the least qualified? Are its procedures fair in rating potential nominees? To what extent should the ABA be involved? After almost forty years of ABA participation in judicial selection, these questions remain unanswered.[1]

The ABA's Standing Committee on Federal Judiciary, which reviews the qualifications of potential nominees, has long been criticized for not having on its committee women, blacks, and solo practitioners, while being biased toward conservative corporate lawyers.[2] Joel Grossman's study in the mid-1960s raised that issue and the concern about how much influence a private organization should have on judicial appointments.[3] In a 1987 poll of lawyers, however, over half thought that the ABA should be "more assertive."[4] But others argue against it. Philip Kurland, for example, questions whether the ABA should play a role in judicial selection at all: "Since the bar is anything but a representative political body, it affords no legitimating function in this regard."[5]

The ABA is now under attack from New Right senators and conservative groups—such as the Washington Legal Foundation and the Judicial Reform Project—that charge it with a "liberal mentality" and contend that its ratings forced Reagan's Justice Department to abandon nominations of the likes of former chairman of the Legal Services Corporation William Harvey and the Office of Management and Budget's general counsel Michael Horowitz. The attack crystallized with a lawsuit by Paul

81

Kamenar, executive director of the Washington Legal Foundation, who claims that the ABA is an "advisory committee" and that its confidential meetings and records violate the Federal Advisory Committee Act. Kamenar accused the ABA committee of holding "secret, Star Chamber-like proceedings in collusion with liberal, left-wing groups" and demanded that it open its meetings and records.[6] While the merits of the lawsuit remain uncertain, Kamenar claims victory. In March 1986, Judge Joyce Green dismissed the case on the ground that, under the Federal Advisory Committee Act, the Washington Legal Foundation could only sue the Justice Department, not the ABA.[7]

The ABA is also being pressured by Reagan's Justice Department. While the ABA used to boast that in thirty years presidents had successfully defied its recommendations less than 1 percent of the time, it now disavows influence on judicial selection.[8] Moreover, the ABA has reneged on its policy (adopted during the Carter years) of consulting with organizations like the National Bar Association—the organization of black lawyers in the country—and the Alliance for Justice when investigating nominees.[9] In addition, ABA President Eugene Thomas, under pressure from New Right conservatives and Justice Department officials to drop John Lane, a prominent lawyer in Washington, D.C., refused to reappoint Lane to the ABA committee on the federal judiciary for another three-year term. Thomas acknowledged that he "was concerned about [the Washington Legal Foundation suit] and wanted the program [of judicial screening] saved."[10]

As New Right conservatives mount pressure on the ABA, moderate Republicans and liberal Democrats have not come to its defense. Illinois Senator Paul Simon, among others, says "that the American Bar Association is not maintaining high enough standards in approving Federal Judges."[11] There also is concern over the fact that the ABA does not explain its ratings—particularly for those rated minimally "qualified"; some agree with the Washington Legal Foundation that the ABA's influence is too great to allow it such confidentiality and unaccountability.

In the past, the ABA's participation in judicial selection served two basic purposes. First, its prestige lent legitimacy to appointees while not altering the basic politics of appointments. Second, especially when nominees were found to be unqualified, it served as a "buffer" between the president and the Senate. But the ABA's future role in judicial selection is uncertain. It may turn on how much the ABA is perceived to compromise its standards in the interests of partisanship and on how thoroughly and fairly it is perceived in rating the nominees.

From an Assertive to a Reactive Role

The ABA first asserted its interest in judicial selection in 1908, when its Committee on Professional Ethics proclaimed that, "It is the duty of the Bar to endeavor to prevent political considerations from outweighing judicial fitness in the selection of Judges."[12] In fact, however, the ABA hoped to defend its own ideological orientation and interests. Between 1878 and the late 1930s, the ABA perceived the federal courts as a bastion of defense against progressive legislation and state encroachment on economic rights. The ABA bitterly fought efforts to make judges more popularly accountable by opposing progressives' plans to have judges elected. Six former ABA presidents and former president (and later chief justice) William Howard Taft also led an unsuccessful attack on the 1916 confirmation of Louis Brandeis to the Supreme Court. In their view, Brandeis's "reputation, character, and career" as a progressive and legal reformer made him "not a fit person to be a member of the Court."[13] According to Grossman, the "inevitable 'confusion' between professional qualifications and ideological soundness marked the judicial-selection efforts of the American Bar Association right through to the New Deal period. These efforts . . . were clear and frank attempts to gain a measure of control over the judicial decision-making process."[14]

In the 1940s, the ABA concentrated on reforming the states' elective systems of judicial selection and promoted the idea of "merit selection."[15] In 1946, it created a Special Committee on the (federal) Judiciary, which the following year was authorized "to promote the nomination of competent persons and to oppose the nomination of unfit persons."[16] In 1949, the Standing Committee on Federal Judiciary, as it is now known, was established to review the qualifications of judicial nominees.

From the outset of the committee, the ABA pushed for influence on the selection of federal judges. In 1947, with the appointment of Judge Harold Medina, it claimed victory in promoting a candidate for a nomination.[17] But the ABA's influence was due largely to its close relationship with Republican Senator Alexander Wiley, who chaired the Senate Judiciary Committee from 1946 to 1949. When the Senate changed hands in 1949, Democratic Senator Pat McCarran took over as chair of the Judiciary Committee, and relations with the ABA cooled. While McCarran continued the practice of asking for the ABA's view on nominees, he was "firmly resolved that the bar associations shall not choose the judiciary of this country."[18] Thus the ABA's initial success in gaining a role in judicial selection was due, in large measure, to its ties with

Republican senators. When the Democrats held sway in the Senate after 1949, the ABA's participation was reduced to occasionally supplying lists of potential nominees to the Justice Department.

It was not until 1951 that the ABA found any solid supporters in the Truman administration. At that time, Attorney General J. Howard McGrath was under fire for failing to prosecute cases of tax evasion, and the administration was under fire for being soft on Communists. McGrath resigned and Truman replaced him with former federal judge James McGranery, who put Ross Malone (formerly on the ABA's board of governors) in charge of judgeships. Malone invited the ABA's recommendations on judges and pushed the idea of the Justice Department's soliciting the ABA's views before sending nominations on to the Senate. Their idea was not put into practice, however, because McGranery decided to withhold all nominations until after the fall 1952 presidential election. Thus only in the last three years of the Truman administration did the ABA enjoy the ear of the Senate Judiciary Committee and the Justice Department. And even so, it could claim success in promoting only a few candidates. Of the forty-nine judges confirmed in those years, the ABA recommended eighteen, considered thirteen to have been "outstanding," and opposed three of the five that the Senate rejected.

When Eisenhower came into office, the ABA's connection with the Justice Department was formalized. Attorney General Herbert Brownell told the ABA committee: "I will continue the program promulgated by Mr. Malone. I think it is a very good one, but I think one aspect of it ought to be eliminated. . . . I do not think the committee ought to be recommending anybody, because then its investigating and reporting functions will be suspect."[19] The ABA agreed to forgo a role in recommending nominees and to consider only one name per vacancy, as well as to forgo a say on Supreme Court nominations.

It was not until 1956, when Bernard Segal assumed chairmanship of the ABA's committee on the federal judiciary, that the administration agreed to let it rate nominees for the country's highest tribunal. Segal also got the Eisenhower administration to submit for screening the names of recess and in-house nominees (usually assistant attorneys general). In addition, the administration agreed to give the ABA the names of nominees at the same time it gave them to the FBI. Prior to that time, the ABA received the names of nominees only after the FBI already conducted its investigation and, as Segal recollects, they were "practically frozen. . . . Unless we could virtually prove . . . 'a high crime and misdemeanor,' we had little hope of stopping the nomination."[20] In return for being provided the names of potential nominees earlier in the process, Segal agreed to give the administration an "informal" evaluation—simply telling the attorney general whether the nominee would be found "qualified" or not. After Lawrence Walsh became deputy attorney general, Segal, who enjoyed great respect within the Eisenhower Justice Department, won agreement on being able to evaluate more than one name for each vacancy. That did not last long, however; since the Kennedy administration, the ABA has generally received only one name for each vacancy.

The ABA's Standards and Ratings

In 1956, when the ABA first rated Supreme Court nominees, there were only two ratings: "qualified" or "unqualified." This rating system prevailed until 1970, when the ABA was severely criticized for approving of Nixon's unsuccessful nominations of Clement F. Haynsworth, Jr., and G. Harrold Carswell. Lawrence Walsh, then ABA Committee on Federal Judiciary chairman, announced that henceforth nominees would be rated as "highly qualified," "not opposed," or "not qualified"— implicitly acknowledging that, prior to that time, virtually anyone nominated got at least a "qualified" rating.

Since 1958, the ABA has rated lower-court nominees as "exceptionally well qualified," "well qualified," "qualified," or "not qualified." The highest rating is for a nominee who "stand[s] at the top of the legal profession in the community involved and [has] outstanding legal ability, wide experience and the highest reputation for integrity and temperament." "Well qualified" nominees "have the Committee's strong affirmative endorsement and [are] regarded as one of the best available for the vacancy from the standpoint of competence, integrity and temperament." The ABA's ratings of lower federal court appointees from the Eisenhower through the Reagan administrations are shown in Table 5.1. It is clear from the table that the ABA increasingly finds fewer nominees either "exceptionally well qualified" or "not qualified."

The response to an ABA rating of "unqualified" has varied from administration to administration. The Kennedy administration, for example, gave much less weight to the ABA than did the Eisenhower administration. In its first two years, the Kennedy administration named eight judges that the ABA deemed "not qualified." At the 1962 ABA convention, deputy attorney general Nicholas deB. Katzenbach "reminded" the ABA "that the responsibility is the President's and the

Table 5.1

ABA Ratings of Judicial Appointees from Eisenhower through Reagan

District Court Judges

ABA Rating	Eisenhower*	Kennedy*	Johnson	Nixon	Ford	Carter	Reagan
Number appointed	125	103	122	179	52	202	225
Exceptionally Well Qualified	17.1%	10.6%	7.4%	4.8%	0%	4.0%	5.3%
Well Qualified	44.6	45.6	40.9	40.4	46.1	47.0	45.8
Qualified	32.6	31.5	49.2	54.8	53.8	47.5	48.8
Not Qualified	5.7	6.3	2.5	0	0	1.5	0

Table 5.1 *(continued)*

Courts of Appeals Judges

ABA Rating	Eisenhower*	Kennedy*	Johnson	Nixon	Ford	Carter	Reagan
Number appointed	45	21	40	45	12	57	66
Exceptionally Well Qualified			27.5%	15.7%	16.7%	16.1%	15.2%
Well Qualified			47.5	57.8	41.7	58.9	37.9
Qualified			20.0	26.7	33.3	25.0	46.9
Not Qualified			2.5				
No Report Requested			2.5				

*The percentages given for Eisenhower and Kennedy are for the total number of judges—not divided into district and appellate judges. These data are from H. Chase, *Federal Judges: The Appointing Process* (Minneapolis: University of Minnesota Press, 1972), p. 168. The data for Johnson through Carter appointees comes from S. Goldman, "Carter's judicial appointments: a lasting legacy," *Judicature* 64 (1981), p. 344. The data on Reagan judges (through 1986) was supplied by the American Bar Association.

Senate's, and this Association does not have and would not wish to have veto power over the appointments to be made."[21] By contrast, Nixon's deputy attorney general, Richard Kleindienst, announced in 1969 that the ABA would have an absolute veto over all lower-court nominees found unqualified. On the other hand, former Connecticut governor Thomas Meskill, nominated for Court of Appeals for the Second Circuit by Nixon in 1974, despite strong opposition from the ABA, eventually won confirmation after being renominated by President Ford.[22] While Carter's attorney general, Griffin Bell, worked with the ABA, his successor Benjamin Civiletti went ahead in 1980 with a couple of nominations of black judges who were opposed—with mixed success—by the ABA.[23] The Reagan administration nominated Sherman Unger as a favor to Nixon—despite the ABA's opposition. (Unger died before his confirmation, and thus Reagan has not appointed any judges rated "not qualified" by the ABA.)[24]

No less critical than the question of ratings is the question of standards—that is whether (and, if so, how far)—the ABA bends to pressure when it rates nominees as "qualified." Liberal organizations contend that the ABA Committee on Federal Judiciary increasingly gave Reagan nominees "qualified" ratings, even though they did not meet its guidelines and were considered "not qualified" by a minority of the committee. The Alliance for Justice charges that "there has been a distinct drop in the quality of the nominees for the Courts of Appeals in the second term of the Reagan Administration . . . which may be a result of the increasingly ideological selection process" and the fact that, although the nominees were not opposed, a minority of the ABA committee voted to rate almost one-third of them as unqualified.[25]

Until the Senate changed hands in 1986, Reagan put up many highly controversial nominees. And the ABA Committee on Federal Judiciary increasingly had a split vote when rating Reagan's appellate court nominees as "qualified." Table 5.2 compares the ratings of Carter and Reagan appellate judges and shows the greater number of Reagan judges rated "qualified" by a split vote of the ABA committee (sixteen as compared to three). Notably, half of the appellate judges put up by Attorney General Meese and rushed through the Republican Senate by Strom Thurmond were given the ABA's lowest ranking of "qualified" and a third by a split vote. By contrast, after the Senate changed hands and the administration named few controversial conservatives in early 1987, only one nominee was rated "qualified" by a split vote, and the rest were unanimously found "qualified" or "well qualified."

Table 5.2

Comparison of Carter and Reagan Courts of Appeals Judges Rated by a Split Vote of the ABA

ABA Rating	Carter Judges	Reagan Judges Total	Under Reagan's Attorneys General Smith	Meese
Exceptionally Well Qualified	8 (14.0%)	10 (15.2%)	7 (21.2%)	3 (9.0%)
Well Qualified	35 (61.4%)	25 (37.9%)	13 (39.4%)	12 (36.6%)
Qualified	11 (19.3%)	15 (22.7%)	8 (24.2%)	7 (21.2%)
Qualified/ Not Qualified	3 (5.3%)	16 (24.2%)	5 (15.1%)	11 (33.3%)
Not Qualified	—	—	—	—

Data supplied by the American Bar Association.

Members of the ABA committee on the federal judiciary deny being pressured directly by the Reagan administration into rating nominees as "qualified." Some former committee members point out that recent chairmen, who have not considered unanimity to be as important as others, have not worked to achieve greater consensus within the committee.

There is no doubt, however, that the ABA has and does—and inevitably must—bend to administrations in order to preserve its role in judicial selection. Pressures to yield have become greater, though, in recent years, since administrations have employed judicial selection to vigorously pursue their legal-policy goals.

Thus, when the Carter administration announced its "affirmative action" policy, the ABA bent on its requirement that nominees must have fifteen years of prior legal experience. Attorney General Bell persuaded the ABA to lower its standard to twelve years so that the administration could name more blacks and women, who, because of professional discrimination and fewer career opportunities, tended to have less legal experience than the traditional white male nominee. The ABA remained "flexible," even on that standard, recalls Brooksley Born—the first woman to serve on the ABA committee (1977-80) and to chair it (1981-83). Eleven out of thirteen Carter nominees with less than twelve years of legal experience were given "qualified" or better ratings. The eleven included four females (one of whom was black), two black males, and three Hispanic males.

The ABA committee bent again—but in a different direction—with the Reagan administration. The administration now not only opposes Carter's "affirmative action" policy, but actively seeks young, white male conservatives who share the administration's legal-policy goals.[26] Reagan has named more younger appellate judges than any prior president, and the ABA has bent its standard of twelve years of prior legal experience for some of these appointments too.

The extent to which the Reagan administration achieved its aims and the ABA bent its standards is reflected in the number of appellate judges who have been appointed at ages under forty. Less than 2 percent of those appointed by Eisenhower, Kennedy, or Johnson were under forty. Three percent (two out of fifty-nine) of Carter's appellate judges were under forty; one was a black male, the other a white female. By comparison, 10 percent of Reagan's appellate judges are under forty; two (one black, one white) are female, the rest white males.[27] Over half of Reagan's under-forty appellate court nominees were rated "qualified" by only a majority of the ABA committee.

The problems with the ABA bending on its standards were publicized when a controversy arose over its rating J. Harvie Wilkinson as "qualified." Wilkinson had no trial experience and less than twelve years of legal experience. Nonetheless, a majority of the ABA committee rated him "qualified" on the basis of his scholarly publications and clerkship for Justice Lewis F. Powell, Jr. He also had worked in the Reagan Justice Department for two years. The controversy grew when it was revealed that, after an initially unfavorable report, Wilkinson had Justice Powell (among others) contact members of the ABA committee in his support.[28] The appearance of the ABA bending to political pressures and of "double standards" loomed larger a year later when, in part because he had only eleven years of legal experience, the ABA initially rated James Spencer, a black, as "unqualified." Spencer, who was eventually confirmed for a district court judgeship, had been nominated by Reagan only after a concerted effort by Senator John Warner to win the first appointment of a black federal judge in the state of Virginia.[29]

Tensions between the ABA and the Justice Department over the age of nominees are long-standing. Though the battle now is over rating younger and less-experienced nominees as "qualified," twenty years ago it was over appointing those who were over sixty. The ABA had a rule that candidates over the age of sixty must be rated "not qualified" for reason of their age. But in 1961, at the insistence of Vice President Johnson and over ABA opposition, the Kennedy administration named Sarah T. Hughes, a widely respected Texas judge who was over the sixty-year age limit. In this case, political support prevailed.

A number of other distinguished individuals, however, were passed over due in part to being rated "not qualified" for reasons of their age. In 1979, for example, the ABA rated Archibald Cox, a respected Harvard Law School professor and special prosecutor during the Watergate investigation, as "not qualified" because he was over the age limit. Again, though, politics played a greater role than the ABA rating—this time to defeat the nomination. Carter refused to nominate Cox because his primary supporter was Senator Edward Kennedy, who had decided to run against Carter in the presidential primary.[30] Nonetheless, as a result of the ABA's rating of Cox, the Senate and the House of Representatives passed resolutions in 1980 urging the ABA to stop discriminating against nominees on the basis of age. In 1981, the ABA abandoned its age criteria for rating judicial nominees.[31]

Over the past forty years, as the ABA committee has bowed to political pressures and bent its standards, it has sacrificed its (always limited) role in promoting highly qualified judicial candidates and become more of a rubber stamp for nominees. The ABA "filters out the extremes," in Philip Lacovara's words.[32] As former attorney general Edward Levi notes, "it does not do much in getting at the best; its major influence is negative, rather than positive."[33] And even so, the ABA's major role lies in attempting to deter nominations rather than in fighting confirmations. The ABA simply cannot overcome strong presidential or senatorial backing of nominees.

The extent to which the ABA succeeds in persuading administrations not to go ahead with nominations is not clear, however. "It's hard to estimate," says Born. According to Robert Raven, another former chair of the ABA Committee on Federal Judiciary (1977-80), "It's not a high percentage figure, although that's where we do our best work."[34]

When the ABA started making so-called informal evaluations—preliminary reports to the Justice Department based on one committee member's investigations, but without the full committee's vote—Grossman thought it would give "the Committee a more significant role in the selection process." Though "it still could not exert much influence at the key recruitment stage," Grossman concluded that the committee "assumed a more creative role [and] was able to begin to fulfill one of the major objectives of the ABA: to promote the nomination of the persons it considered best qualified."[35]

Chairmen of the ABA Committee on Federal Judiciary have claimed that there were times when a high percentage of potential nominees who were initially rated unqualified were screened out by the ABA. Robert Trescher, for one, estimated that about 20 percent of the prospective nominees were found "not qualified" in the ABA's initial screening and subsequently not nominated by the president.[36] Harold Chase, who studied judicial recruitment during the Kennedy administration, estimated that a substantial percentage of the ABA's initial ratings were negative—though he also found that a number were upgraded before the ABA's final evaluation and their nomination for appointment.[37]

Recent chairmen of the ABA committee, however, deny major influence on the selection of nominees. They also deny that ratings are frequently changed between the initial and final evaluations. Bernard Segal, for example, claimed that "in 95 percent of the cases (I am guessing), the eventual rating in the full committee's formal report is the same as the preliminary informal report."[38] Robert Raven concurs: "In the five years that I've been on the committee [a change in rating] hasn't happened one percent of the time."[39]

Whether the ABA committee ever exercised the kind of influence that Grossman and Chase claimed in the 1960s and that New Right critics allege it does now appears improbable. Carter's Attorney General Griffin Bell recalls that in over two hundred appointments, the ABA initially found only "ten or twelve" to be "not qualified"—and subsequently the ABA gave "five or six of them qualified ratings."[40] Born contends that during the Carter years, the role of the ABA changed to that of "a post-selection check."[41] Bruce Fein claims that during the Reagan administration, the ABA had "difficulties with less than one out of 20 nominees."[42]

The Standing Committee on Federal Judiciary

The ABA's Standing Committee on Federal Judiciary does not actively promote, in Justice Antonin Scalia's words, "the best and the brightest." It tends to rate virtually all nominees as either "well qualified" or "qualified." That reflects both pressures brought to bear on the committee and self-imposed constraints intended to preserve its role in judicial selection. No less important, though, in accounting for the committee's reactive rather than assertive role are the limitations of the committee's investigations and ratings. As the number of judicial nominees has increased, those on the committee (which has not changed in size) have had to bear ever greater burdens. And as the committee's workload increases, its deliberations and the thoroughness of its investigations may slip—thereby contributing to more split votes on nominees.

The makeup of the committee also predisposes it to approve virtually all nominees. The committee is composed of fourteen members, the chairman and one representative for each judicial circuit in the country. Each representative is appointed on a staggered basis by the president of the ABA and serves (without being paid) for a three-year term and a possible three-year reappointment. Most committee members come from large law firms; Born is the only woman to have served on the committee, and only in recent years have blacks and Hispanics served. A long-standing criticism is that the committee is not even representative of the ABA, which itself represents less than half of the legal profession.

Numerous other criticisms have focused on how the committee investigates potential nominees—particularly the fact that the informal evaluation is based only on the investigation of the judicial circuit representative. This process has been described by former Democratic Senator Abraham Ribicoff as "one man's fiat" and a committee's rubber stamp.[43] Since only the circuit representative is responsible for an investigation, the investigations are inexorably uneven—contingent on the time, resources, and dedication of individual committee members— and open to the possibility of unchecked bias and prejudice. And just as New Right critics charge the ABA with a liberal bias, liberal groups— particularly black organizations like the NBA and the NAACP Legal Defense Fund—have long complained that the ABA is too conservative and that individual committee members occasionally reveal prejudice.

In response to such criticism, and after controversy over three nominations in 1980, the ABA modified its procedures. In part, the controversy was over the "not qualified" ranking given to two black attorneys, U. W. Clemon and Fred Gray, nominated for courts in the South. The Senate Judiciary Committee raised serious questions about the fairness of the ratings and the thoroughness of the ABA's investigations. Ultimately, Clemon, though not Gray, was confirmed. Controversy also arose over lower-court nominee Charles Winberry, Jr. Initially, the ABA rated him "qualified"; then it reversed itself. The Senate Judiciary Committee rejected his nomination. Since these controversies, when a circuit representative determines that a nominee does not merit at least a "qualified" rating, then a second member of the Committee on Federal Judiciary is immediately assigned to investigate the candidate as well.

While this reform promotes fairer and more thorough investigations, it reinforces the tendency to rate the vast majority of candidates as "qualified" and for informal ratings of circuit representatives to determine the whole committee's final rating. Between 1977 and 1984, for instance, the ABA Committee on Federal Judiciary investigated a total of 502 judicial candidates, and 465 were eventually given a formal rating. Of those 465 candidates, 30 were rated "exceptionally well qualified," 212 were rated "well qualified," and 212 were rated "qualified." Only 11 were deemed "not qualified"; 6 of those were nominated and 3 subsequently confirmed.[44]

Conclusion

The ABA does not play an assertive role in promoting the best qualified for the federal bench and has no role in the initial recruitment process. At best, the ABA helps to exclude the most objectionable and to set minimum standards for those serving on the federal bench.

Both the method and standards for the ABA's rating of judicial nominees will continue to draw fire from New Right conservatives and liberals alike. For one thing, both the New Right and liberals agree that the process of nominating and confirming judges should be open to a broader range of interest groups. According to Yale law school professor and former Ralph Nader employee Peter Schuck, "If the ABA is to have the privilege of partnership in the nominating process—an extraordinary delegation of public power to a private organization—other interest groups should also be encouraged to participate, for their views of the nominee's qualifications may be at least as informative and relevant as those of the ABA."[45] In addition, both New Right conservatives and liberals would like the ABA to explain its reasons for rating nominees as "not qualified."

Beyond these criticisms, the tendency of the ABA to rate virtually all nominees as "qualified" remains troubling. To overcome this problem, the ABA might shift to a system of rating candidates as either "well qualified" or "not qualified"—thereby forcing harder choices. Alternatively, a system of "pass/no pass" could be adopted, but this would not go nearly as far in altering current practices.

· 6 ·

Conclusion:
The Politics of
Federal Judgeships

I T IS THE SWING of electoral politics that largely determines who
makes it to the federal bench. Party affiliation remains the controlling consideration. During any presidency, potential candidates identified with the party out of power are virtually excluded from the pool
of contenders. Other traditions work to exclude or underrepresent
segments of the population. As a result, the federal judiciary is neither
a meritocracy nor expressly representative of the general public.

Still, despite the premium on political accommodation, judgeships are
not simply a matter of either presidential or senatorial patronage. The
nominating and confirmation process imposes a kind of internal check.
The political bargaining that ensues has, at times, resulted in some bad
appointments—usually due to deals struck in deference to either presidential or senatorial patronage. But in this century—particularly since the
era of New Deal judges and the American Bar Association's involvement in judicial selection—professional qualifications have been taken
more seriously, and the quality of the federal bench has generally
improved.

Presidents weigh patronage, professional considerations, and their own
legal-policy goals differently when selecting nominees. All administrations seek party faithful, but both Carter and Reagan gave less weight
to professional qualifications than to their own legal-policy goals. In different ways and for different reasons, each pressured the ABA to bend
its standards for nominees—Carter seeking to bring racial, gender, and
ethnic diversity to the federal bench, Reagan to appoint those sharing
his philosophy of judicial conservatism.

There are those in both political parties—especially Democratic and moderate Republican senators—who object to the assertion of greater presidential control over the selection of lower federal court judges and to the emphasis on promoting legal-policy goals through judicial selection. Yet even the fiercest critics agree that the president is free to nominate whom he wants based on his own priorities—even if ideological goals are placed above professional considerations and political patronage.

Recent debate over the Reagan administration's judicial selection—that is, over the priority given its legal-policy goals—is in some respects misguided. Reagan's goals differ only in degree from those of past administrations. FDR, for example, primarily appointed supporters of his New Deal program. The real break with past recruitment practices and policies lies in the Reagan administration's reorganization of the selection process within the Justice Department and establishment of greater White House oversight, more rigorous screening, and questioning of potential nominees to ascertain their agreement with the goals of the administration.

The administration's efforts to remold the judiciary in light of its own legal-policy agenda are facilitated by senatorial patronage and institutional disincentives for scrutinizing and challenging nominees. Most nominations simply receive rubber-stamp approval. This is especially so when the chairman of the Senate Judiciary Committee has an ideological affinity with the president. It was thus during Senator Strom Thurmond's chairmanship of the Judiciary Committee that the Reagan administration made its most controversial lower-court appointments. By contrast, when Democratic Senator Joseph Biden assumed chairmanship of the committee, with over sixty vacancies on the federal bench, the administration made only thirty-one nominations and the Senate voted to confirm only ten in the first five months of 1987. Justice Department officials agree with Senate staff and other close observers that more controversial and conservative nominees who won approval under Senator Thurmond would now be neither nominated nor confirmed.[1]

Critics argue that judicial selection has become too politicized and too ideological and that there must be a better way to appoint judges. In 1986, for instance, New York's Governor Mario Cuomo suggested that "a better way to choose judges is to rescind from ideology, party, so-called political philosophy, and use instead what for lack of a more meritorious label we call the 'merit' criteria. I think the American Bar Association criteria, the criteria in the Constitution and statutes of the state of New York, and the writings of the Founding Fathers, all wisely leave out ideology, philosophy and party. Instead, irreproachable integrity, experience, wisdom, knowledge of the law, judicial temperament, collegiality where appropriate, and ability to communicate orally and in writing are fit criteria, and all we need."[2] Cuomo, thereupon, endorsed the idea of nonpartisan judicial nominating commissions—which New York and some other states have—to recommend judicial candidates who are appointed by the governor.

The idea of creating a national judicial nominating commission is not new. Opposition to the Warren Court's rulings on desegregation and the rights of the accused prompted numerous proposals to take judicial recruitment out of the hands of the Justice Department and into those of a "nonpartisan" commission.[3] In particular, the American Bar Association in 1958 adopted a resolution recommending the creation of such a commission, but it failed to win the Eisenhower administration over to the idea.[4] Almost a decade later, Senator Hugh Scott championed another such proposal.[5] Along with the ABA, the American Judicature Society and others (including some judges) have since endorsed the idea as a way to get higher-quality appointments.[6]

Such proposals do not fare well, because they would cut back on the patronage of either the president, the Senate, or both.[7] Also, studies of similar state judicial nominating commissions, and Carter's so-called merit commissions, demonstrate that politics is not eliminated.[8] Instead, elected officials share power over judicial selection with representatives of bar associations and other interest groups. That is not to say that a national judicial nominating commission might not improve the quality of the federal bench. Rather, depending on the structure of such a commission, the configuration of the politics of judicial selection would simply change—for better or worse.

There remains, however, a strong argument for not modifying the impact that shifts in electoral politics have on the selection of federal judges. For it is through the swing of presidential and congressional elections and the vested interests of the president and the Senate in appointing judges that federal courts are generally held accountable and historically aligned with the country.

No less controversial is the idea of establishing nonpartisan standards for judicial appointments. But the concept of judicial "merit" is elusive (it is difficult to attain precision and bipartisan agreement on definitions), and political pressure to bend standards is great. Further, the history of the politics of judicial selection demonstrates that presidents may set their own standards—occasionally even contrary to popular and professional opinion—and that the Senate's standards are parochial, individually and partisan-based.

Major reform of the politics of judicial selection or an elusive quest for precise nonpartisan standards is not realistic. More promising for improving the quality of the federal bench are procedural changes. While it remains unlikely that administrations will look beyond the pool of party faithful for judicial candidates, the appointment process could be made more open to public scrutiny. When nominations are made, interest groups should have adequate notification, time to conduct their own investigations, and the opportunity to present findings to the Senate Judiciary Committee. The committee itself should allow time (at least three weeks) for investigating nominees' backgrounds before holding confirmation hearings. Even more important, the committee must allocate more resources for independent staff investigations—particularly now that more than fifty judgeships are annually conferred. If the ABA is to play a more constructive role in the future, it must stop rating virtually all nominees as "qualified" and provide explanations for its unfavorable ratings. Through these changes, the politics of appointing federal judges should become more visible, accessible, and publicly accountable.

Epilogue:
The Bork Controversy

T HE CONTROVERSY over President Ronald Reagan's nomination of Judge Robert H. Bork to the Supreme Court illustrates the extent to which the judicial appointment process has become politicized.

Bork was the twenty-seventh Supreme Court nominee to be rejected and forced to withdraw due to Senate opposition; he was the fifth nominee in this century to be defeated for political reasons. In 1930, President Herbert Hoover's nominee, Judge John J. Parker, went down by a vote of 39 to 41; in 1969 and 1970, two of Richard M. Nixon's nominees— Judges Clement F. Haynsworth, Jr., and G. Harrold Carswell—were defeated; in 1968, after mustering a 45 to 43 vote but failing to obtain the two-thirds needed to end a filibuster led by Republicans and conservative southern Democrats, Justice Abe Fortas withdrew from consideration to replace Chief Justice Earl Warren.

The controversy that presaged Bork's defeat was rooted in the Justice Department's ambitious agenda for judicial reform and was part of its plan to have the federal judiciary carry "the Reagan Revolution"—that is, his conservative social agenda and a free-market economic philosophy—into the next century.[1] From the outset of the Reagan administration, judgeships were viewed as symbols and instruments of presidential power; they were campaign issues in 1980, 1984, and during the 1986 congressional elections.

Reagan's naming of Bork, one of the Supreme Court's sharpest critics and a jurist in the vanguard against regulation and antitrust enforcement, proved the catalyst to a political fire storm. Both the White House and the Justice Department made clear that Bork's confirmation—viewed as a way to reassert presidential strength badly damaged by the Iran-contra affair—was a top priority in the waning days of the Reagan administration.[2] But the administration clearly underestimated the opposition that would be touched off by the nomination and by the loss of a Republican majority in the Senate after the 1986 elections. Reagan had campaigned for Republicans in the Senate race, including five in the South, but all lost to Democrats. The conservative southern Democrats, in particular, were thus not inclined to be counted as allies of the administration and the New Right in a confirmation battle that raised the issue of race and civil rights.

Because of rumors that Bork—who had been passed over three times before, by President Ford in 1975 and by Reagan in 1981 and 1986—would be given the next seat on the Supreme Court, liberal interest groups were well prepared to fight his confirmation.[3] Senators Edward Kennedy and Joseph Biden (chairman of the Judiciary Committee) immediately denounced Bork. More than eighty-three liberal organizations, ranging from the National Organization for Women to the United Mine Workers, followed. The American Civil Liberties Union, which had only once before opposed a Supreme Court nominee (William H. Rehnquist in 1971), called Bork "unfit" to serve on the high bench. And promising a "no-holds-barred battle," the AFL-CIO, which had not opposed a nomination since Haynsworth and Carswell, also came out against Bork's confirmation.[4]

The mobilization of interest groups was not confined to anti-Bork forces. New Right organizations were active as well during the atypical seventy-day period between the nomination and confirmation hearings. The Moral Majority, American Conservative Union, American Life League, and Concerned Women for America all joined in, although without the fervor of the liberals.

Initially, the White House discouraged aggressive support of Bork by the New Right. Instead, the White House aimed to downplay Bork's views on civil liberties and to recast Bork, an outspoken and controversial conservative, as a "centrist" jurist. In a speech given on July 29, Reagan equated Bork's judicial philosophy with that of the recently retired Justice Lewis F. Powell, Jr.,—despite Bork's attacks on Powell's opinions. A 70-page White House briefing book was prepared, followed by a 240-page report released by the Justice Department portraying Bork as a mainstream jurist.[5]

The White House's strategy angered some New Right supporters. Patrick McGuigan, for one, head of the conservative Coalition for America, was irritated that the White House staff repeatedly rebuffed suggestions for an "August offensive" on behalf of Bork. By late September, though, when Bork appeared in trouble, the White House adopted a stronger line of attack. The president made a personal appeal to the public: "Tell your senators to resist politicization of our court system. Tell them you support the appointment of Judge Bork."[6] New Right supporters launched major newspaper and letter-writing campaigns. The range of debate was unprecedented. Within weeks, more than 250 op-ed articles on Bork (pro and con) appeared in over 200 newspapers. Over fifteen reports—mostly critical—were distributed by special-interest groups to editorial boards around the country. The staff of the Democrat-controlled Judiciary Committee issued its own seventy-two-page study refuting the administration's depiction of Bork as a "centrist."

For special-interest groups and consultants on the left and right, Bork was a bonanza. As Roger Gravers, a direct-mail consultant, put it: "This is equivalent of Jim Watt wanting to flood the Grand Canyon."[7] The People for the American Way, a liberal group founded by television producer Norman Lear, launched a $2 million media campaign. The National Conservative Political Action Committee alone committed over $1 million to help push the Bork nomination through the Senate. Although conservative special-interest groups found fund-raising more difficult than their liberal counterparts, Senate offices were inundated with mail that resulted from letter-writing campaigns orchestrated by pro-life groups and fundamentalists.

The People for the American Way's television spots, starring Gregory Peck, drew particular criticism for politicizing the process and denigrating the nominee and the Court. The television spots actually appeared in only a small number of markets; some stations refused to air them for fear they might have to give Bork's supporters equal time. Reagan, however, drew national attention to the spots by denouncing them as "miscast."[8] Utah's Republican Senator Orrin Hatch took time during the televised hearings to repeatedly criticize the spots as part of "a dirty tricks campaign."

While the media campaigns were unprecedented, the mobilization of special-interest groups was not. In the 1930s, labor unions and civil rights groups joined together in a campaign that defeated Judge Parker on the grounds that he was antilabor and opposed black voting rights. However demeaning for the nominee and the Court, given the influence of the media and the growing political role of consultants and political action committees, such special-interest-group participation appears inevitable.

The media campaigns—aimed at influencing public opinion and thereby the twenty-five or so undecided senators—had more apparent than real significance in the end. They served to dramatize the event and the choice facing the Senate, but it was clear by the start of the third week of the confirmation hearings that few senators were moved—except to decry the activities of special-interest groups on both sides. What ultimately had far greater impact was Bork's own philosophy and his role in both the preconfirmation fray and the confirmation proceedings.

Even before the Judiciary Committee began its hearings, Bork took the unusual step of granting a large number of interviews to all of the major newspapers. This both broke with tradition and gave the appearance of participating in a public relations campaign. In the past, nominees refrained from courting press coverage. For example, in 1911, when asked by a reporter for *The Baltimore Sun* whether he would respond to charges against him, Louis Brandeis observed, "I have not said anything and will not. . . .and that goes for all time and to all newspapers, including both the *Sun* and the moon."[9] Like Brandeis, Bork faced charges of being a "radical." Unlike Brandeis and other prior nominees who let their records speak for themselves, Bork sought to explain, clarify, and amend his twenty-five-year record as law professor, solicitor general, and judge.[10]

Although the White House had discouraged Bork from giving interviews, by the time the hearings began in mid-September it settled on "letting Bork be Bork."[11] This initially appealed to the major television networks. ABC and NBC expected Bork to come off like a "judicial Ollie North." The Bork hearings, though, didn't come close to the Iran-contra hearings held in the same room earlier in the summer. After Bork's first day of testimony, the commercial networks stopped coverage. Only some channels of the Public Broadcasting System, Cable News Network, and C-SPAN continued to broadcast them (in the evenings).

Bork's lengthy explanations of his record—and his attempt to refashion himself as a moderate, even a "centrist" jurist[12]—also were unprecedented. In Vermont Democratic Senator Patrick Leahy's words, the issue became "confirmation conversion"—whether Bork was "born again." Bork surpassed all previous nominees in discussing controversial issues. He also gave assurances on how he would vote in the future. Pennsylvania's Republican Senator Arlen Specter and Arizona's Democratic Senator Dennis DeConcini extracted promises (or concessions) on the First Amendment, the Fourteenth Amendment's equal protection clause, the commerce clause, and issues like abortion and gender discrimination. While judges have appeared as witnesses for themselves during confirmation hearings since Harlan F. Stone did so in 1925, all previous Supreme Court nominees have refused to answer questions about their views on specific cases and controversies, let alone reveal how they might vote on issues coming before the Court.

Bork not only downplayed his long-standing criticism of the Court's rulings as "theoretical" disagreements but, under pressure from the Judiciary Committee's questioning, said that he "was about where the Supreme Court is" on the First and Fourteenth Amendments. "The law is settled in *Brandenburg [v. Ohio]*. . . . As a judge I accept [it]." As much as anything else, Bork tried to assure all that he had "no ideological agenda" and "a great respect for precedent." That proved difficult because of his record of assailing so many watershed rulings in the past thirty years and his repeated declarations that "in the field of constitutional law, precedent is not all that important."[13] Bork nevertheless claimed that he had abandoned his earlier views and, time and again, said he was "about where the Supreme Court is." As for upholding precedent, he vowed, "I'm not going to undo. . . anything that's been done."

By the time Bork finished testifying, he had contradicted many of his earlier written opinions—opinions for which he had been nominated in the first place. And candor, as much as judicial philosophy, became a major issue. Specter observed a "considerable difference between what Judge Bork has written and what he has testified he will do if confirmed as an associate justice." Even Bork apparently felt it necessary at the conclusion of his five days of testimony to attempt to assure the Senate by stating, "It really would be preposterous to say things I said to you and then get on the Court and do the opposite. I would be disgraced in history."[14]

More than the media hype and special-interest-group activities, more than the 110 witnesses assembled for and against him, Bork's performance weighed the most heavily in the final decision. As one Judiciary Committee aide noted before the vote took place, "The Bork testimony is clearly 80 to 90 percent of the decision."[15] Thomas Korologos, the Washington lobbyist who advised Bork and the White House on confirmation strategy, agreed that Bork's testimony failed to persuade; it was like "two trains passing in the night up there—communication level was zero."[16]

Other participants in the confirmation process also contributed to the campaign-politics atmosphere. For the first time, a former president, Gerald Ford, introduced and recommended a nominee to the Judiciary Committee. On the final day of the hearings, Biden read a letter from former president Jimmy Carter, expressing opposition to Bork and disagreement with the testimony of two of his administration's top officials—Attorney General Griffin Bell and legal counsel Lloyd Cutler.

While William Howard Taft, among other presidents, had privately pushed nominees before, no president had publicly sided with—or testified for—them.

Nor have justices, especially sitting justices, ever before come out as allies of a president or his nominee—until the Bork controversy. Retired Chief Justice Warren E. Burger proclaimed Bork "the most qualified nominee of the last fifty years." Justices John Paul Stevens and Byron R. White publicly endorsed Bork at the outset of the hearings.[17] In addition, a parade of former attorneys general, cabinet officials, senators, and law professors testified for and against Bork, underscoring how politicized the appointment process had become.

What is particularly disturbing is that the witnesses generally appeared as advocates (either for or against Bork) rather than as expert witnesses on Bork's legal qualifications. The testimony of such witnesses as artist Robert Rauschenberg and Pulitzer Prize-winning author William Styron (in opposition) and conservative black economist Thomas Sowell (in support) was irrelevant—except to attract publicity. Democrats on the Judiciary Committee realized this sooner than the administration. After the opening testimony by Barbara Jordan (black former congresswoman) and William Coleman (a prominent black Republican and Ford's secretary of transportation), they cut short a long list of representatives of liberal groups that were to testify, so as to let Bork's testimony stand on its own.

In the end, the debate centered on what kind of Constitution we have. Is it "the Founders' Constitution"—identified with Attorney General Meese's call for a "jurisprudence of original intention" and repeatedly defended by Bork in his testimony?[18] Or is such reliance on the Founders' "intentions" unduly restrictive and an incomplete guide for constitutional interpretation? Seen in terms of a debate on the Constitution, the hearings came closer than any before to a national debate—in Biden's words, "a referendum on the past progress of the Supreme Court and a referendum on the future."[19]

What most captured attention at the end of three weeks of hearings were public opinion polls running against Bork's confirmation. Shortly before the week of October 5, when the Senate Judiciary Committee voted nine to five to recommend that the Senate reject Bork's confirmation, a *Washington Post*/ABC News poll found that 52 percent of the public opposed confirmation. Another poll—conducted by the *Atlanta Constitution*—of twelve southern states revealed that 51 percent of its respondents were against Bork; even white conservatives opposed him by 44 to 39 percent.[20]

Bork's supporters, not surprisingly, decried the influence of public opinion. In Hatch's words, "This has become a freak sideshow." Bork himself issued a public statement, "Federal judges are not appointed to decide cases according to the latest opinion polls. . . . [When nominees] are treated as political candidates. . .the effect will be to erode public confidence and endanger the independence of the judiciary."[21]

But it is questionable whether Bork's defeat can be attributed to public opinion polls. As Biden stated before the Judiciary Committee voted on October 6, "We belittle this institution and the American people [by suggesting] the conclusion reached by our colleagues was the result of a handful of interest groups spending $1 million to hoodwink us all."[22] Senators and their staffs had spent an entire summer examining Bork's record and considering his professional reputation. The Judiciary Committee's hearings and examination was more thorough than that given to the overwhelming majority of all judicial nominees. There was ample basis for the Senate to assess Bork's record, reputation, and judicial philosophy.

To be sure, the activities of pressure groups figured into Bork's defeat. Within a few days of the Judiciary Committee's vote, seven conservative southern Democrats, led by Louisiana's Senator J. Bennett Johnston, announced their opposition to Bork. This, along with similar announcements by Republican Senator Specter and conservative Democratic Senator DeConcini, pushed the two remaining Democrats on the Judiciary Committee—West Virginia's Robert Byrd and Alabama's Howell Heflin— to abandon their view that the committee ought not make any recommendation. As a result, the vote was nine to five, with only the remaining Republican senators supporting Bork.[23]

But the most important strategy in any confirmation battle has always been that of marshaling Senate forces in support or in opposition. The process is now just more open and wide-ranging than it was twenty or fifty years ago. And it always is more difficult and complex when nominees are associated with a controversial political agenda.

Bork was nominated and rejected (by the widest margin ever, 58 to 42) because he was perceived as an instrument for achieving the New Right's political agenda. That is what the debate over the Constitution during the committee's hearings was about. It is what turned not only conservative southern Democrats but six moderate Republican senators against him.

Even after Bork's defeat, though, Attorney General Meese and Assistant Attorney General William Bradford Reynolds pressured Reagan to turn to Judge Douglas H. Ginsburg—another ideological conservative.[24] But disclosures about Ginsburg's personal life, which outraged the New Right's constituency, soon forced his withdrawal.[25]

Thus, while the Senate is predisposed to defer to a president's Supreme Court nominations, controversies are certain to follow when nominees are cast as symbols of presidential power and instruments for achieving some narrow political agenda. At bottom, this is what the recent controversy was about. It was not a controversy between Republicans and Democrats, or even conservatives and liberals, per se. It was a controversy that pitted the New Right against traditional conservatives and advocates of judicial self-restraint in both parties. That badly politicized the confirmation process and denigrated the Court. But nominees ought not to be associated with some special-interest group's political agenda; judges should not represent narrow political constituencies. For that is at war with the Constitution and the tradition of judicial independence. And it undermines public confidence in the judiciary and the idea of "a government of laws, not of men."

Appendix A

QUESTIONS BY THE HONORABLE JEREMIAH DENTON
AND HONORABLE JOHN P. EAST
to Andrew L. Frey, Nominee to the
District of Columbia Court of Appeals

1. Do you believe that the Constitution guarantees a "right to privacy"? If so, please indicate the constitutional sources of that right, its precise nature and its limitations.

2. (a) In his dissent to the majority opinion of the Supreme Court in *Roe v. Wade,* 410 U.S. 113 (1973), Justice Byron R. White made the following statement: "As an exercise of raw judicial power the Court perhaps has authority to do what it does today, but in my view its judgment is an improvident and extravagant exercise of the power of judicial review which the Constitution extends to this court." Do you agree or disagree with Justice White's statement? Why or why not?

(b) In his dissent to the same Roe opinion, Justice William H. Rehnquist made the following statement: "The decision here to break the term of pregnancy into three distinct terms and to outline the permissible restrictions the state may impose upon each one partakes more of judicial legislation than it does of the determination of the intent of the drafters of the Fourteenth Amendment." Do you agree or disagree with this statement? Why or why not?

3. (a) In *Roe v. Wade,* the Supreme Court determined that even the "viable" unborn human fetus is not a "person" as that term is used in the Fifth and Fourteenth Amendment to the Constitution. Do you believe that a "viable" fetus is a human being? If so, do you agree with the Court's finding that the "viable" fetus is not a "person"? If so, on what basis can a valid constitutional distinction be drawn between a "human being" and a "person"?

(b) Is a child who is born alive after an abortion a "person" under the Fifth and Fourteenth Amendments? Does the "right to an abortion" that the Court created with its Roe decision have any application after a child is born alive as the result of an abortion?

(c) Is a handicapped, or severely handicapped, child born alive a "person" under the Fifth and Fourteenth Amendments to the Constitution?

4. (a) Does the "right to privacy" from which the *Roe v. Wade* abortion privacy doctrine of the Supreme Court is derived have any application to any right of the parent of a handicapped newborn child to decide whether to provide him or her with life-saving medical care, and/or ordinary care in the form of nutritional sustenance and liquids (whether by natural or intravenous means)? If so, why? If not, why not?

(b) Do you believe that legislation ever can be held to be invalid because those who enacted it did so based on the belief that the conduct proscribed is morally wrong, or that an activity or institution encouraged or helped by the legislation is morally right? What difference, if any, does it make whether such moral beliefs are based on a belief in the existence of a Supreme Being?

5. In 1972 the Supreme Court in *Furman v. Georgia* 408 U.S. 238, struck down federal and state death penalty statutes that allowed for unguided discretion by the trier of fact to determine whether or not the death penalty should be imposed. On February 22, 1984, through the able leadership of the distinguished Chairman of this Committee, the Senate passed by a vote of 63-32, S. 1765, a bill to establish constitutional procedures for the imposition of the sentence of death for certain federal offenses. What is your view on the death penalty?

6. The Department of Justice recently noted that the number of prisoners challenging the validity of their state convictions through federal habeas corpus petitions rose nearly 700 percent from 1961 through 1982, but only a small number of inmates were successful in gaining any type of release. In an attempt to control the flow of frivolous collateral attacks on a criminal defendant's convictions, the Senate, again through the able leadership of Chairman Thurmond, passed on February 6, 1984, S. 1763, a bill to reform current habeas corpus procedures.

In your view, should any limits be placed on criminal defendant's ability to collaterally attack this conviction? If so, what are the limits?

7. On February 7, 1984, the Senate passed S. 1764, a bill which limits the use of the Exclusionary Rule by providing that evidence obtained in a search or seizure and which is otherwise admissible as evidence will not be excluded in a federal trial if the search or seizure was undertaken in a reasonable, good faith belief that it conformed to the Fourth Amendment.

Do you believe that there should be any limits placed on the use of the Exclusionary Rule? If so, do you believe that S. 1764 or this type of limitation is appropriate?

8. The First Amendment forbids the establishment of a State religion. The First Amendment also prohibits interference with the free exercise of religion. This second prohibition apparently is often overlooked. Please share with the Committee your views on the free exercise clause as it relates to prayer in public schools.

9. Is it unconstitutional for state or local governments to give tuition vouchers to parents of all children who attend nonpublic schools? Does it make any difference whether most of these children attend religious schools, provided that the law makes no distinction between religious and nonreligious schools?

10. The Second Amendment to the Constitution states that "a well-regulated militia being necessary to the security of a free state, the right of the people to keep and bear arms shall not be infringed." In light of that constitutional prohibition, to what extent, if any, do you feel that Congress could curtail the right of the people to keep and bear weapons that are of value to common defense?

11. Would you give your present personal position with regards to the Equal Rights Amendment?

12. (a) What did the Supreme Court hold in *Regents of the University of California v. Bakke,* 438 U.S. 256 (1978)? Do you believe that this holding was correct? Why or why not?

(b) In his dissent to the majority opinion on the Supreme Court in *Fullilove v. Klutznick,* 448 U.S. 448, S37-S48, (1980), Justice John Paul Stevens noted that the compelling government interest of curing the effects of past racial discrimination will justify a class-based infringement of the legitimate interests and expectations of innocent third parties only to the extent necessary to restore proven discriminatees to the position they would have occupied in the absence of the discrimination. What role should affirmative action-type remedies take in dealing with individuals who have not been the victims of discriminatory practices?

13. (a) Do you believe that *Brown v. Board of Education,* 347 U.S. 483 (1954), was correctly decided? What disagreements, if any, do you have with the language or reasoning of the Court's decision in that case?

(b) Do you believe that *Swann v. Charlotte-Mecklenburg Board of Education,* 402 U.S. 1 (1971), was decided correctly? If so, do you believe that there is a conflict or tension between the constitutional right to color-blind treatment that was announced in *Brown* and the right (or, if it makes a difference, the remedy) of race-conscious school assignment that was announced in *Swann?* If so, how do you reconcile this tension or conflict?

14. (a) What limitations, if any, do you believe there are on the constitutional power of Congress to enact exceptions to the jurisdiction of the Federal courts and regulations of this jurisdiction?

(b) What are the sources of these limitations?

15. Section 9 (a) of the National Labor Relations Act states: Representatives designated or selected for the purposes of collective bargaining by the majority of the employees in a union appropriate for such purposes shall be the exclusive representatives of all the employees in such a unit for the purposes of collective bargaining in respect to rates of pay, wages, hours of employment or other conditions of employment. . . Keeping in mind that unions are private

associations rather than governments, do you think that the granting of exclusive representation powers to unions by the National Labor Relations Act is unconstitutional?

16. Do you concur with the Supreme Court's decisions in *Abood v. Detroit Board of Education* and *Ellis/Fails* that mandatory service fees collected from non-union members under the jurisdiction of an exclusive bargaining agent can only be used to pay direct collective bargaining and grievance administration costs?

17. In *United States v. Enmons*, the Supreme Court affirmed a District Court ruling that the Hobbs Act did not prohibit the use of violence in obtaining legitimate union objectives. What is your analysis of the *Enmons* decision?

QUESTIONS BY THE HONORABLE JEREMIAH DENTON AND HONORABLE JOHN P. EAST
for the Nomination Hearing of Andrew L. Frey,
to be Judge of the District of Columbia Court of Appeals

1. Please explain your view of whether the Bill of Rights, or rights in general, protect citizens or governments?

What do you think the Founding Fathers thought they were doing when they wrote the Second Amendment to the U.S. Constitution?

What do you think the Second Amendment means? Why?

2. Do you believe the use of force for protection should be legal?

If legal, should one be able to own the means for protection? Incorporate in your response the restrictions on the use of shotguns and rifles in the District of Columbia.

Note, a survey commissioned by an anti-handgun organization has found that 9 percent of handgun-owning households report having used a handgun for protection from a criminal within the past five years, which works out to at least 1.7 million adults. Comment on the results of this study.

3. Mr. Frey, given your membership in an organization which advocates banning the possession of handguns (The National Coalition to Ban Handguns, Inc.) and your statements that you favor regulations to control handgun ownership, would you disqualify yourself, because of bias, in any case involving the District of Columbia firearms statutes should you be confirmed?

If not, please explain.

4. As a Republican nominee do you support the provisions of the Republican Platform on firearms as recently adopted in Dallas?

If not, why not?

5. Please elaborate on your views on (a) mandatory penalties for the use of a firearm in the commission of a crime, approved by the voters in the District of Columbia in 1982, (b) mandatory penalties for possession/transportation of firearms.

6. In order to take away a person's firearms after dismissal/acquittal, it was necessary to overturn many years of precedent. Do you believe that persons who have had their firearms confiscated and then the charges dropped or they are acquitted, should have their firearms returned?

If not, why not?

What are your views on the confiscation of firearms absent specific legislation allowing such action?

7. Many have questioned your membership and donations to gun control groups. Some assume you therefore would have a predisposition against firearms cases that would come before you.

A judge should hear courteously, answer wisely, consider soberly and judge impartially.

What specific readings of law review articles, books, papers and other documents can you cite to show your knowledge of firearms issues that would contribute to your impartiality?

Appendix B

*ABA PERSONAL DATA QUESTIONNAIRE
FOR CANDIDATES WHO ARE ALREADY JUDGES*

In answering these questions, please use letter size paper. Repeat each question and place your answers immediately beneath it. To expedite matters, send in your completed Questionnaire as soon as possible, since it is a prerequisite for the usual process of investigation.

1. Full name and social security number.
2. Office and home addresses, zip codes, telephone numbers and area codes.
3. Date and place of birth.
4. Are you a naturalized citizen? If so, give date and place of naturalization.
5. Family status:
    a) Are you married? If so, state the date of marriage and your spouse's full name including maiden name if applicable.
    b) Have you been divorced? If so, give particulars, including the date, the name of the moving party, the number of the case, the court, and the grounds.
    c) Names of your children, with age, address and present occupation of each.
6. Have you had any military service? If so, give dates, branch of service, rank or rate, serial number and present status.
7. List each college and law school you attended, including dates of attendance, the degrees awarded and, if you left any institution without receiving degree, the reason for leaving.
8. List of courts in which you have been admitted to practice, with dates of admission. Give the same information for administrative bodies which require special admission to practice.

113

9. Describe chronologically your law practice and experience after your graduation from law school and until you became a judge, including:

    a) whether you served as clerk to a judge, and if so, the name of the judge, the court, and the dates of the period you were a clerk.

    b) whether you practiced alone, and if so, the addresses and the dates.

    c) the dates, names and addresses of law firms or offices, companies, or governmental agencies with which you have been connected, and the nature of your connection with each.

    d) any other relevant particulars.

10.   a) What was the general character of your practice before you became a judge, dividing it into periods with dates if its character changed over the years.

    b) Describe your typical former clients, and mention the areas, if any, in which you specialized.

11.   a) Did you appear in court regularly, occasionally or not at all? If the frequency of your appearances in court varied, describe each such variance, giving dates.

    b) What percentage of these appearances was in

        1) Federal courts.

        2) State courts of record.

        3) Other courts.

    c) What percentage of your litigation was

        1) Civil.

        2) Criminal.

    d) State the number of cases in courts of record you tried to verdict or judgment (rather than settled), indicating whether you were sole counsel, chief counsel, or associate counsel.

    e) What percentage of these trials was

        1) Jury.

        2) Non-jury.

    f) Describe ten of the most significant litigated matters which you personally handled and give the citations, if the cases were reported. Give a capsule summary of the substance of each case, and a succinct statement of what you believe to be the particular significance of the case. Identify the party or parties whom you represented; describe in detail the nature of your participation in the litigation and the final disposition of the case. Also state as to each case a) the dates of the trial period or periods, b) the name of the court and the name of the judge before whom the case was tried, and c) the individual name, address and telephone numbers of co-counsel and of counsel for each of the other parties.

12. State the judicial office you now hold, and the judicial offices you have previously held, giving dates and the details, including the courts involved,

whether elected or appointed, periods of service and a description of the jurisdiction of each of such courts with any limitations upon the jurisdiction of each court.

13. Describe ten of the most significant opinions you have written, or attach copies of them to your answers, and give the citations if the opinions were reported, as well as citations to any appellate review of such opinions.

14. Have you ever held public office other than a judicial office? If so, give the details, including the offices involved, whether elected or appointed and the length of your service, giving dates.

15. Have you ever been an unsuccessful candidate for elective, judicial, or other public office? If so, give details, including dates.

16. Have you ever been engaged in any occupation, business, or profession other than the practice of law or holding judicial or other public office? If so, give details, including dates.

17. Are you now an officer or director or otherwise engaged in the management of any business enterprise?

    a) If so, give details, including the name of the enterprise, the nature of the business, the title or other description of your position, the nature of your duties and the term of your service.

    b) Is it your intention to resign such positions and withdraw from any participation in the management of any such enterprises if you are nominated and confirmed? If not, give reasons.

18. Have you ever been arrested, charged, or held by federal, state, or other law enforcement authorities for violation of any federal law or regulation, county or municipal law, regulation or ordinance? If so, give details. Do not include traffic violations for which a fine of $50.00 or less was imposed.

19. Have you, to your knowledge, ever been under federal, state or local investigation for possible violation of a criminal statute? If so, give particulars.

20. Has a tax lien or other collection procedure ever been instituted against you by federal, state or local authorities? If so, give particulars.

21. Have you ever been sued by a client or a party? If so, give particulars.

22. Have you ever been a party or otherwise involved in any other legal proceedings? If so, give the particulars. Do not list proceedings in which you were merely a guardian ad litem or stakeholder. Include all legal proceedings in which you were a party in interest, a material witness, were named as a co-conspirator or a co-respondent, and any grand jury investigation in which you appeared as a witness.

23. Have you ever been disciplined or cited for a breach of ethics or unprofessional conduct by, or been the subject of a complaint to, any court, administrative agency, bar association, disciplinary committee, or other professional group? If so, give the particulars.

24. With respect to your judicial service,

    a) Have you participated in any proceeding in which you had a personal or other financial interest in one of the parties or in the matter in controversy? If so, give particulars.

b) Is there a rule or custom in your court as to judges sitting on such cases? If so, state the rule or custom and whether or not you have complied with it.

c) Have you to the best of your knowledge and belief complied with applicable statutes and Canons of the American Bar Association relative to such matters as were in force and applicable at the time? If not, give particulars.

d) Have you ever received compensation from outside sources for services rendered (other than fees or expenses for lectures or teaching)? If so, give particulars.

25. a) What is the present state of your health?

b) Have you in the last 10 years (i) been hospitalized due to injury or illness or (ii) been prevented from working due to injury or illness or otherwise incapacitated for a period in excess of ten days? If so, give the particulars, including the causes, the dates, the places of confinement, and the present status of the conditions which caused the confinement or incapacitation.

c) Do you suffer from any impairment of eyesight or hearing or any other physical handicap? If so, give details.

d) When did you have your most recent general physical examination, and who was the supervising physician?

e) Are you currently under treatment for an illness or physical condition? If so, give details.

f) Have you ever been treated for or had any problem with alcoholism or any related condition associated with consumption of alcoholic beverages or any other form of drug addiction or dependency? If so, give details.

g) Have you ever been treated for or suffered from any form of mental illness? If so, give details.

26. Furnish at least five examples of legal articles, books, briefs, or other legal writings which reflect your personal work. If briefs are submitted, indicate the degree to which they represent your personal work.

27. a) List all bar associations and professional societies of which you are or have been a member and give the titles and dates of any offices which you have held in such groups.

b) List also chairmanships of any committees in bar associations and professional societies, and memberships on any committees which you believe to be of particular significance (e.g., judicial selection committee, committee of censors, grievance committee).

c) Describe also your participation, if any, on judicial committees, in judicial conferences, and in sitting, by designation, as a temporary member of the court which reviews decisions of your court.

28. List all organizations other than bar associations or professional societies of which you are or have been a member, including civic, charitable, religious, educational, social and fraternal organizations.

29. List any honors, prizes, awards or other forms of recognition which you have received (including any indication of academic distinction in college or law school) other than those mentioned in answers to the foregoing questions.

30. State any other information which may reflect positively or adversely on you, or which you believe should be disclosed in connection with consideration of you for nomination for the Federal Judiciary.

_____

Signature

_____

Date

U.S. DEPARTMENT OF JUSTICE
QUESTIONNAIRE FOR JUDICIAL CANDIDATES

A. NAME AND POSITION

1. Name: (include any former names used)
2. Government position for which you are under consideration.
3. Address: List current residence address and mailing address.
4. List all office and home telephone numbers where you may be reached.
5. Marital status: If married, identify spouse's present employer and spouse's employer for the five preceding years.
6. List all jobs held in the past 10 years, including the title or description of job, name of employer, location of work, and dates of inclusive employment.

B. PERSONAL DATA

1. Have your federal or state tax returns been the subject of any audit or investigation or inquiry at any time? If so, explain.
2. Are you currently under federal, state, or local investigation for a possible violation of a criminal statute? If so, please give full details.
3. List all memberships and offices held in professional, fraternal, scholarly and civic organizations.
4. Have you ever been disciplined or cited for a breach of ethics or unprofessional conduct by, or been the subject of a complaint to, any court, administrative agency, professional association disciplinary committee, or other professional group? If so, please give full details.

5. Have you ever been involved in civil litigation, or administrative or legislative proceedings of any kind, either as plaintiff, defendant, respondent, witness or party in interest, which may be appropriate for consideration by the Committee of the Senate to which your nomination will be submitted? If so, please give full details.

6. List all offices with a political party held during the past 10 years. List any public office for which you have been a candidate during the past 10 years.

7. List all contributions to political parties or election committees during the past 6 years.

8. What is the condition of your health?

9. Have you had a physical examination recently?

10. Without details, is there or has there been anything in your personal life which you feel, if known, may be of embarrassment to the Administration in the event you should be nominated? What about any near relative?

C. FINANCIAL DATA

Please note that federal law and regulations governing conflicts of interest require Presidential appointees within 30 days of their entrance on duty to provide reports of specified financial interests as to themselves, their spouses and any other member of their immediate households. The initial four matters listed below are designed to elicit financial information similar to—although, in some cases, broader in scope—than that which all Presidential appointees are required to provide by Executive Order of the President. The remaining paragraphs in this section seek elaboration on your financial status beyond that which the existing Executive Order and regulations require. The information which you provide will not be transmitted to the Senate Committee considering your nomination, or otherwise be made public, without your consent. As to all matters, please provide the requested information for yourself, your spouse, minor children and any other member of the immediate household.

1. List the names of all corporations, companies, firms, or other business enterprises, partnerships, nonprofit organizations, and education or other institutions—

(A) with which you are now connected as an employee, officer, owner, director, trustee, partner, advisor, attorney, or consultant. (Attorneys and consultants need list only their major clients, but should include all of those whom you represent on a regular basis or which might give rise to an appearance of bias on your part in connection with your proposed appointment);

(B) in which you have any continuing financial interests, through a pension or retirement plan, stock bonus, shared income, severance pay agreement, or otherwise as a result of any current or prior employment or business or professional association. As to each financial arrangement, provide all details necessary for a thorough understanding of the way in which the arrangement operates, including information concerning any renewal right you may have if the arrangement is allowed to lapse and whether lump sum or severance benefits are available in lieu of continuation of the interest; (C) in which you have any financial interest through the ownership of stocks, stock options, bonds, partnership interests, or other securities. Any interests held indirectly through trusts or other arrangements should be included. (Please provide a copy of any trust or other agreement.)

2. Provide a complete, current financial net worth statement that itemizes in detail:
(A) the identity and value of all assets held, directly or indirectly. This itemization should include, but not be limited to, bank accounts, real estate, securities, trusts, investments and other financial holdings;
(B) the identity and amount of each liability owed, directly or indirectly, which is in excess of $1,000. This itemization should include, but not be limited to, debts, mortgages, loans and other financial obligations for which you, your spouse or your dependents have a direct liability or which may be guaranteed by you, your spouse or your dependents. In identifying each liability, indicate the nature of the liability and the entity or person to which it is owed.
A sample net worth statement is attached for your convenience. You may use any form you like.*
(C) List sources and amounts of all items of value received during calendar years 1984 and 1985 (including, but not limited to, salaries, wages, fees, dividends, capital gains or losses, interests, rents, royalties, patents, honoraria, and other gifts other than those of nominal value).
(D) Please provide for review by this office (but not for submission to Senate Committee staff or to the public) copies of your federal income tax returns for the preceding three-year period.

---

*See pp. 121-22.

D. FUTURE EMPLOYMENT RELATIONSHIPS

1. Will you sever all connections with your present employers, business firms, business associations or business organizations, if you are confirmed by the Senate?

2. Do you have any plans, commitments or agreements to pursue outside employment, with or without compensation, during your service with the government? If so, explain.

E. POTENTIAL CONFLICTS OF INTEREST

1. Describe all financial arrangements, stock options, deferred compensation agreements, future benefits and other continuing relationships with business associates, clients or customers.

2. Describe any business relationship, dealing or financial transaction which you have had during the last five years, whether for yourself, on behalf of a client, or acting as an agent, that could in any way constitute or result in a possible conflict of interest in the position to which you have been nominated.

3. Describe any activity during the past five years in which you have engaged for the purpose of directly or indirectly influencing the passage, defeat or modification of any legislation or affecting the administration and execution of law or public policy.

4. Explain how you will resolve any potential conflict of interest, including any that may be disclosed by your responses to the above items.

CONFIDENTIAL FINANCIAL STATEMENT
NET WORTH

Provide a complete, current financial net worth statement which itemizes in detail all assets (including bank accounts, real estate, securities, trusts, investments, and other financial holdings) all liabilities (including debts, mortgages, loans, and other financial obligations) of yourself, your spouse, and other immediate members of your household.

ASSETS

Cash on hand in banks _____

U.S. Government securities—add
    schedule _____

Listed securities—add schedule _____

Unlisted securities—add schedule _____

Accounts and notes receivable:
    Due from relatives and friends _____
    Due from others _____
    Doubtful _____

Real estate owned—add schedule _____

Real estate mortgages receivable _____

Cash value—life insurance _____

Other assets—itemize:

_____ _____

_____ _____

_____ _____

_____ _____

    Total assets _____

LIABILITIES

Notes payable to banks—secured _____
Notes payable to banks—unsecured _____
Notes payable to relatives _____
Notes payable to others _____
Accounts and bills due _____
Unpaid income tax _____
Other unpaid tax and interest _____
Real estate mortgages payable—add
  schedule _____
Chattel mortgages and other liens
  payable _____
Other debts—itemize: _____

    Total liabilities _____
    Net worth _____
    Total liabilities and net worth _____

CONTINGENT LIABILITES

As endorser, comaker or guarantor _____
On leases or contracts _____
Legal claims _____
Provision for Federal Income Tax _____
Other special debt _____

GENERAL INFORMATION

Are any assets pledged? (Add schedule.) _____
Are you defendant in any suits or
  legal actions? _____
Have you ever taken bankruptcy? _____

Notes

Chapter 1

1. Letter to Thomas Reed Powell, Stone Papers, Box 24, Manuscripts Room, Library of Congress, Washington, D.C.

2. Letter of professors Laurence Tribe and Philip Kurland to Senate Judiciary Committee, June 1, 1986 (obtained from the Senate Judiciary Committee).

3. See "Institutions: Confidence Even in Difficult Times," *Public Opinion* (1981), p. 33; Hearst Report, *The American Public, the Media and the Judicial System* (New York: Hearst Corporation, 1983); and W. Murphy, J. Tannenhaus, and D. Kastner, *Public Evaluations of Constitutional Courts: Alternative Explanations* (Beverly Hills, Calif.: Sage, 1973).

4. For examples and further discussion, see D. M. O'Brien, *Storm Center: The Supreme Court in American Politics* (New York: Norton, 1986), pp. 81-85.

5. F. Frankfurter, *From the Diaries of Felix Frankfurter,* ed. by J. Lash (New York: Norton, 1974), p. 155.

6. Quoted and discussed by O'Brien, *Storm Center,* pp. 97-102. Forty-five federal judges have been subject to impeachment proceedings, but only ten faced trials and only five were convicted.

7. See Clark, "Adjudication to Administration: A Statistical Analysis of Federal District Courts in the Twentieth Century," *Southern California Law Review* 55 (1981), p. 65.

8. Figures (as of June 30, 1986) from David Cook, Administrative Office of the United States Courts.

9. Clark, "Adjudication to Administration," pp. 86-88.

10. See, for example, W. McCree, "Bureaucratic Justice: An Early Warning," *University of Pennsylvania Law Review* 129 (1981), p. 777; and P. Higginbotham, "Bureaucracy—The Carcinoma of the Federal Judiciary," *Alabama Law Review* 31 (1980), p. 261.

11. A. Scalia, "Remarks before the Fellows of the American Bar Foundation," New Orleans, Louisiana, February 25, 1987; and D. M. O'Brien, "Clearing the Heft of Cases: Justice Scalia Tries a Plan," *Los Angeles Times,* March 1, 1987, p. 3.

12. See W. Rehnquist, "Year-End Report on the Judiciary," December 31, 1986. And for a discussion of the salaries of judges and lawyers, see R. Posner,

The Federal Courts: Crisis and Reform (Cambridge, Mass.: Harvard University Press, 1985), pp. 33-41.

13. Quoted in M. Cannon and D. M. O'Brien, eds., *Views from the Bench: The Judiciary and Constitutional Politics* (Chatham, N.J.: Chatham House, 1985), p. 29.

14. S. Hufstedler, "Courtship and Other Legal Arts," *American Bar Association Journal* 60 (1974), pp. 545-47.

15. E. Griswold, "The Federal Courts Today and Tomorrow—A Summary and Survey," *University of South Carolina Law Review* 38 (1987), p. 393.

16. See P. Carrington, "The Function of the Civil Appeal: A Late-Century View," *University of South Carolina Law Review* 38 (1987), p. 411.

17. L. Powell, *The Powell Memorandum: Attack on American Free Enterprise* (Washington, D.C.: U.S. Chamber of Commerce, 1971), p. 7.

18. See *Congressional Quarterly Weekly Report* 38, no. 2046 (1980). The 1980 and 1984 Republican party platforms pledged to appoint those "whose judicial philosophy is characterized by the highest regard for protecting the rights of law-abiding citizens. [This] is consistent with the belief in the decentralization of the federal government and efforts to return decision-making power to state and local elected officials [and those] who respect traditional family values and the sanctity of innocent human life."

19. Louis Harris Poll, conducted during the Rehnquist confirmation hearings, based on a representative sample of 1,248 adults across the country. (Made available to the author by Nancy Broff, Judicial Selection Project.)

20. Quoted in D. M. O'Brien, "Meese's Agenda for Ensuring the Reagan Legacy," *Los Angeles Times,* "Opinion," September 28, 1986, p. 3.

21. Based on data supplied by Sheila Joy, Office of the Deputy Attorney General, U.S. Department of Justice. This includes Reagan's appointments through 1986.

22. Tables 1.1, 1.2, and 1.3 are based on materials contained in W. Dornette and R. Cross, *Federal Judicial Almanac 1986* (New York: John Wiley & Sons, 1986), as supplemented by material in D. Rutkus, "Judicial Nominations by President Reagan during the 99th Congress," *Issue Brief* 1119 (Washington, D.C.: Congressional Research Service, Library of Congress, November 5, 1986), and elsewhere.

23. O. Hatch, *Reagan and the Courts* (Washington, D.C.: Washington Legal Foundation, 1980).

24. Telephone interview with Bruce Fein, December 10, 1986.

25. Testimony of H. Schwartz, U.S. Congress, Senate, Committee on the Judiciary, *Confirmation Hearings on Federal Appointments,* 99th Cong., 1st sess., pt. 2, 1985, p. 449. See also H. Schwartz, *The New Right's Court Packing Campaign* (Washington, D.C.: People for the American Way, 1985).

26. C. Stern, "Judging the Judges: The First Two Years of the Reagan Bench," *Benchmark* 1 (1984), p. 1.

27. Ibid., p. 5.

28. Quoted by G. Rees in "Dr. James McClellan," *The Review of the News* (1985), pp. 31, 37.

29. See D. Songer, "Consensual and Nonconsensual Decisions in Unanimous Opinions of the United States Courts of Appeals," *American Journal of Political Science* 26 (May 1982), p. 238; and S. Goldman, "Voting Behavior on the United States Courts of Appeals Revisited," *American Political Science Review* 69 (1975), p. 491.

30. J. Gottschall, "Reagan's appointments to the U.S. Courts of Appeals: the continuation of a judicial revolution," *Judicature* 70, no. 49 (1986), pp. 51-52. See also J. Gottschall, "Carter's judicial appointments: the influence of affirmative action and merit selection on voting on the U.S. Courts of Appeals," *Judicature* 67, no. 165 (1983).

31. C. K. Rowland, D. Songer, and R. Carp, "Presidential Effects on Criminal Justice Policy in the Lower Federal Courts: The Reagan Judges," pp. 22-25 (unpublished paper, 1985; supplied to the author, for which he expresses his appreciation). The study is based on a random sample of 1,122 district court opinions and 1,500 appellate opinions. For a similar study and findings, see: Note, "All the President's Men? A Study of Ronald Reagan's Appointments to the U.S. Court of Appeals," *Columbia Law Review* 87 (1987), p. 101.

Chapter 2

1. See W. Willoughby, *Principles of Judicial Administration* (Washington, D.C.: Brookings Institution, 1929), p. 355; and E. Haynes, *Selection and Tenure of Judges* (Newark, N.J.: National Conference of Judicial Councils, 1944), p. 3.

2. See K. Hall, *The Politics of Justice: Federal Judicial Selection and the Second Party System* (Lincoln: University of Nebraska Press, 1979); and "Letters from the Federal Farmer," in H. Storing, ed., *The Complete Anti-Federalist* (Chicago: University of Chicago, 1981), vol. 2, p. 309.

3. See M. Farrand, *The Records of the Federal Constitution of 1787* (New Haven: Yale University Press, 1911), vol. 1, pp. 119-28, 232-33; vol. 2, pp. 41-44, 80-83, 121, 498-99, 533, 539, and 627-28. J. Elliot, *Elliot's Debates,* 2nd ed. (Philadelphia: J. B. Lippincott, 1941), vol. 1, pp. 174, 209-10, 227, 396, 409, 423, 491; vol. 5, pp. 88, 155-56, 328, 330, 349-50, 379, and 403. See also J. Harris, *The Advice and Consent of the Senate* (Berkeley: University of California Press, 1953).

4. R. Yates, *Secret Proceedings of the Federal Convention* (Richmond, Va.: W. Curtiss, 1839), p. 163; Richard Henry Lee, "The Letters of a Federal Farmer," in Storing, *The Complete Anti-Federalist,* and in P. Ford, *Pamphlets on the Constitution of the United States* (New York: Burt Franklin reprint, 1971), p. 277.

5. Elliot, *Elliot's Debates,* vol. 4, p. 134, and vol. 2, pp. 466-511.

6. A. Hamilton, J. Madison, and J. Jay, *The Federalist Papers,* ed. by C. Rossiter (New York: New American Library, 1961), p. 401.

7. Oral history interview with Robert H. Jackson, transcript p. 729, Robert H. Jackson Papers, Box 19, Library of Congress, Washington, D.C.

8. See, e.g., B. Shartel, "Federal Judges—Appointment, Supervision, and Removal—Some Possibilities Under the Constitution," *Michigan Law Review* 28 (1930), pp. 485, 723, and 870; and S. Markman, "A Comparison of Judicial Selection Procedures" (unpublished office memorandum), U.S. Department of Justice, Office of Legal Policy, 1986.

9. K. Hall, "Why We Don't Elect Federal Judges," *this Constitution* (1985), pp. 20, 26.

10. See C. Warren, *The Supreme Court in United States History* (Boston: Little, Brown, 1922), vol. 1, p. 137; and C. Fish, *The Civil Service and Patronage* (New York: Russell, 1904), p. 24.

11. Quoted by L. Fisher, *Constitutional Conflicts Between Congress and the President* (Princeton: Princeton University Press, 1985), p. 35.

12. B. Shartel, "Federal Judges—Appointment, Supervision, Removal—Some Possibilities Under the Constitution," *Journal of the American Judicature Society* (1931), p. 22.

13. Robert Kennedy Oral History Interview, John F. Kennedy Presidential Library, Waltham, Massachusetts, p. 603. See also, White House Central Files—Federal Government, Boxes 505 and 530, Kennedy Presidential Library; and James Eastland Oral History Interview, Lyndon Baines Johnson Presidential Library, Austin, Texas, pp. 14-15.

14. W. Mitchell, "Appointment of Federal Judges," *American Bar Association Journal* 17 (1931), p. 569. See also, William Mitchell Papers, Box 7, Minnesota Historical Society; and White House Central Files, Box 441, Herbert Hoover Presidential Library, Westbranch, Iowa.

15. See Shartel, "Federal Judges"; Harris, *The Advice and Consent of the Senate* p. 15; H. Chase, "Federal Judges: The Appointing Process," *Minnesota Law Review* 51 (1966), p. 185; and H. Chase, *Federal Judges: The Appointing Process* (Minneapolis: University of Minnesota Press, 1972).

16. Circuit Courts of Appeals Act of 1891, 26 Stat. 826 (1891); and 28 U.S.C. § 133 (1964).

17. District of Columbia Code, Volume 4, Title 11, § 433 and 434 (1981 and 1986 Supplement).

18. Interview with P. Lacovara, October 28, 1986. See also, P. Lacovara, "The Wrong Way to Pick Judges," *The New York Times,* October 3, 1986, p. A36.

19. For a further discussion of the politics of appointing members of the Supreme Court, see D. M. O'Brien, *Storm Center: The Supreme Court in American Politics* (New York: Norton, 1986), pp. 44-80.

20. Harris, *The Advice and Consent of the Senate,* p. 317. See also, J. Schmidhauser, *Justices and Judges: The Federal Appellate Judiciary* (Boston: Little, Brown, 1979); and Hall, *The Politics of Justice,* p. 189.

21. The American Bar Association kept records on the party affiliations of judicial appointees until 1969, when it was no longer deemed important. Percent-

ages here (for Roosevelt to Kennedy) are based on R. Richardson and K. Vines, *The Politics of Federal Courts* (Boston: Little, Brown, 1970), p. 68; and (for Johnson to Reagan) on S. Goldman, "Reaganizing the judiciary: the first term appointments," *Judicature* 68 (1985), p. 313.

22. Memorandum to the President, January 6, 1965, John Macy Papers, Box 726, "Judgeships File," Lyndon Baines Johnson Presidential Library, as quoted in O'Brien, *Storm Center,* p. 44.

23. H. Abraham, "A bench happily filled: some historical reflections on the Supreme Court appointment process," *Judicature* 66 (1983), pp. 282, 286.

24. Based on interviews conducted for O'Brien, *Storm Center.*

25. *Jacobellis v. Ohio,* 378 U.S. 184, 197 (1964).

26. W. Schaefer, "Good Judges, Better Judges, Best Judges," *Journal of the American Judicature Society* 44 (1960), pp. 22, 23.

27. Quoted in J. Goulden, *The Benchwarmers* (New York: Random House, 1974), p. 37.

28. Quoted in "Here Come the Judges," *Time,* December 11, 1978, p. 112; and "Merit Selection Chances Improve," *Congressional Quarterly Weekly Report,* February 18, 1978, pp. 393-94.

29. For further discussion, see O'Brien, *Storm Center,* pp. 47-51.

30. J. W. Howard, *Courts of Appeals in the Federal Judicial System* (Princeton: Princeton University Press, 1981), p. 90

31. D. Jackson, *Judges* (New York: Atheneum, 1974), pp. 255, 258.

32. Howard, *Courts of Appeals,* p. 99.

33. Schmidhauser, *Justices and Judges,* p. 96.

34. This data was obtained from the Office of the Deputy Attorney General, U.S. Department of Justice, Washington, D.C.

35. T. Uhlman, "Race, Recruitment and Representation: Background Differences Between Black and White Trial Court Judges," *Western Political Quarterly* 30 (1977), pp. 457, 462.

36. L. Berkson, "Women and the bench: a brief history," *Judicature* 65 (1982), pp. 286, 289. See also, S. Carbon, P. Houlden, and L. Berkson, "Women on the state bench: their characteristics and attitudes about judicial selection," *Judicature* 65 (1982), p. 294; and B. Cook, "Women as Supreme Court candidates: from Frances Allen to Sandra O'Connor," *Judicature* 65 (1982), p. 314.

37. C. Epstein, *Women in the Law* (New York: Basic Books, 1981), p. 179.

38. See E. Slotnick, "The paths to the federal bench: gender, race and judicial recruitment," *Judicature* 67 (1984), pp. 371, 387. See also, E. Martin, "Women on the federal bench: a comparative profile," *Judicature* 65 (1982), p. 306.

39. S. Goldman, "Carter's judicial appointments: a lasting legacy," *Judicature* 64 (1981), p. 344.

40. B. Cook, "Political Culture and Selection of Women Judges in Trial Courts," in Stewart, ed., *Women in Local Politics* (Metuchen, N.J.: Scarecrow Press, 1980), pp. 42, 49-50.

41. See, e.g., B. McM. Wright, "A Black Broods on Black Judges," *Judicature* 57 (1973), p. 22. See also, R. Marcus, "For Black Lawyers, Path to Top is Slow," *The Washington Post,* November 16, 1986, p. Al.

42. S. Goldman, "Should there be affirmative action for the judiciary?" *Judicature* 62 (1979), pp. 489, 493. See also, G. Kessler, "Affirmative Action Can Mean the Best Person for the Job," *The Judges Journal* 22 (1984), p. 12; and R. Davidow, "Judicial Selection: The Search For Quality and Representativeness," *Case Western Reserve Law Review* 31 (1981), p. 409.

43. For a discussion of Roosevelt's appointments, see O'Brien, *Storm Center,* pp. 59, 67-75; and Memorandum In Re Supreme Court, President's Secretary's Files, Box 186, Franklin Roosevelt Presidential Library, Hyde Park, New York.

44. See, e.g., Memorandum for the President: Re New Judgeships on the Ninth Circuit Court of Appeals, June 17, 1968, White House Central Files— Federal Government, Executive Files, Box 505, File 8; Memorandum from Larry Temple to the President, July 10, 1968, Box 505, File 10; Larry Temple Papers, Box 1, Memoranda on July 11, 17, and 30, 1968 (pertaining to vacancies on the Fifth, Sixth, and Ninth appellate courts); and Barefoot Sanders Papers, Box 8, Memorandum of March 18, 1967 (on the appointment of Harrold Carswell to the Fifth Circuit), all at the Lyndon Baines Johnson Presidential Library.

45. Note on telephone conversation with Attorney General Herbert Brownell, September 9, 1956, Dwight David Eisenhower Diaries, Box 11, Dwight Eisenhower Presidential Library, Abilene, Kansas.

46. See Schmidhauser, *Justices and Judges,* p. 64.

47. Data on the Roosevelt appointees is taken from "Comparative List Showing Religion of Judges," Francis Biddle Papers, Box 2, Franklin Roosevelt Presidential Library; and that for other presidents from S. Goldman and T. Jahnige, *The Federal Courts as a Political System,* 3rd ed. (New York: Harper & Row, 1985), Table 3.1, p. 54. (The percentage given for Reagan's appointees is only for his first term in office.)

48. See material in Francis Biddle's papers, Roosevelt Presidential Library; and Memorandum for the Attorney General, November 27, 1942, Box 2, Roosevelt Presidential Library.

49. See J. Dolan, Oral History Interview, John Kennedy Presidential Library, p. 84.

50. For further discussion, see O'Brien, *Storm Center,* p. 63.

51. R. Nixon, *RN: The Memoirs of Richard Nixon* (New York: Grosset & Dunlap, 1978), p. 423. See also file on Lillie in Records of the Department of Justice, National Archives and Records Service, Washington, D.C.

Chapter 3
1. See H. Cummings and C. McFarland, *Federal Justice* (New York: Macmillan, 1937), p. 527.

2. J. Grossman, *Lawyers and Judges: The ABA and the Politics of Judicial Selection* (New York: John Wiley & Sons, 1965), p. 25.

3. R. Soloman, "The Politics of Appointment and the Federal Courts' Role in Regulating America: U.S. Courts of Appeals Judgeships from T.R. to F.D.R.," *American Bar Foundation Research Journal* (1984), p. 285.

4. R. Burke, "The Path to the Court: A Study of Federal Judicial Appointments" (unpublished dissertation, Vanderbilt University, Nashville, Tenn., 1958), p. 13.

5. For a discussion of FDR's appointments to the Supreme Court, see D. M. O'Brien, *Storm Center: The Supreme Court in American Politics* (New York: W. W. Norton, 1986), pp. 67-76.

6. Letter, May 6, 1940, Robert Jackson Papers, Box 87, Library of Congress, Washington, D.C.

7. Oral History Interview with Robert Jackson, Robert Jackson Papers, Box 19, Library of Congress, Washington, D.C., p. 729.

8. See, for example, letters to Harlan Stone when serving as attorney general under President Herbert Hoover. Harlan Stone Papers, Box 43, Library of Congress, Washington, D.C. See also papers of Attorney General William Mitchell, Minnesota Historical Society, St. Paul, Minnesota.

9. See papers of Felix Frankfurter, Harvard Law School, Cambridge, Mass., and Library of Congress, Washington, D.C.

10. Oral History Interview with Robert Jackson, p. 734.

11. See *Congressional Record* 96, p. 12,104 (1950); *Congressional Record* 97, p. 12,838 (1951); and J. Harris, *The Advice and Consent of the Senate* (Berkeley: University of California Press, 1953), p. 321.

12. Letter, March 28, 1955, Dwight David Eisenhower Diaries, Box 10, Dwight Eisenhower Presidential Library, Abilene, Kans.

13. See S. Goldman, "Characteristics of Eisenhower and Kennedy Appointees to the Lower Federal Courts," *Western Political Quarterly* 755 (1965); S. Goldman, "Judicial Appointments to the United States Courts of Appeals," *Wisconsin Law Review* 186 (1967); H. Chase, *Federal Judges: The Appointing Process* (Minneapolis: University of Minnesota Press, 1972), pp. 90-119; and J. Gottschall, "Eisenhower's Judicial Legacy," *Legal Studies Forum* 9 (1985), p. 251.

14. Interview with Herbert Brownell, November 12, 1986. Lawrence Walsh expressed similar views in an interview with National Public Radio, "All Things Considered," August 28, 1985.

15. W. Rogers, "Judicial Appointments in the Eisenhower Administration," *Journal of the American Judicature Society* 41 (1957), p. 38.

16. Quoted in D. Jackson, *Judges* (New York: Atheneum, 1974), p. 244.

17. V. Navasky, *Kennedy Justice* (New York: Atheneum, 1971), p. 244.

18. J. Goulden, *The Benchwarmers* (New York: Random House, 1974), pp. 62-63.

19. See Chase, *Federal Judges;* H. Chase, "The Johnson Administration—Judicial Appointments 1963-66," *Minnesota Law Review* 52, (1968), p. 965; and A. Neff, *The United States District Judge Nominating Commissions: Their Members, Procedures and Candidates* (Chicago: American Judicature Society, 1981), p. 19.

20. N. McFeeley, *Appointment of Judges: The Johnson Presidency* (Austin: University of Texas Press, 1987).

21. Quoted in ibid., p. 54.

22. For an extensive discussion of Johnson's relationship with Justice Fortas, see O'Brien, *Storm Center,* pp. 84-100. See also R. Carp and C. K. Rowland, *Policymaking and Politics in the Federal District Courts* (Knoxville: University of Tennessee Press, 1983), pp. 60-61.

23. McFeeley, *Appointment of Judges,* pp. 38-41.

24. Quoted in "The Judiciary: Nixon Nearing Record on Nominees," *Congressional Quarterly Weekly Report,* December 16, 1972, p. 3,158.

25. See S. Markman, "A Comparison of Judicial Selection Procedures," Memorandum for Attorney General Edwin Meese, September 8, 1986 (unpublished manuscript in the possession of the author, also based on conversations with Justice Department officials at the time).

26. Quoted by R. Evans, Jr., and R. Novack, *Nixon in the White House* (New York: Random House, 1971), p. 166.

27. Markman, "A Comparison of Judicial Selection Procedures."

28. Ibid., p. 25.

29. Ibid., p. 26.

30. G. Ford, "Attorney General Edward H. Levi," *University of Chicago Law Review* 52 (1985), p. 284.

31. Telephone interview with Edward Levi, December 19, 1986. Other sources for this discussion include a telephone interview with Phil Modlin, December 9, 1986; materials in Edward Schmultz's papers, Box 7, and White House Central Files in the Gerald Ford Presidential Library, Ann Arbor, Michigan.

32. Quoted by H. Abraham, *The Judicial Process* (New York: Oxford University Press, 1986), pp. 31-32.

33. See G. Fowler, "Judicial selection under Reagan and Carter: a comparison of their initial recommendation procedures," *Judicature* 67 (1984), p. 266; and A. Neff, "Breaking with tradition: a study of the U.S. District Judge Nominating Commission," *Judicature* 64 (1981), p. 258.

34. Executive Order 11972.

35. Executive Order 12097.

36. See L. Berkson and S. Carbon, *The United States Circuit Judge Nominating Commission: Its Members, Procedures and Candidates* (Chicago: American Judicature Society, 1980); and A. Neff, *The United States District Judge Nominating Commissions: Their Members, Procedures and Candidates* (Chicago: American Judicature Society, 1981). See also, J. Tydings, "Merit

selection for district judges," *Judicature* 61 (1977), p. 113; J. Rosenbaum, "Implementing federal merit selection," *Judicature* 61 (1977), p. 125; S. Levinson, "U.S. Judges: The Case for Politics," *The Nation,* March 4, 1978, p. 228; P. Fish, "Merit Selection and Politics," *Wake Forest Law Review* 15 (1979), p. 635; E. Slotnick, "The U.S. Judge Nominating Commission," *Law & Society Quarterly* 1 (1979), p. 465; and E. Slotnick, "Lowering the Bench or Raising it Higher?: Affirmative Action and Judicial Selection During the Carter Administration," *Yale Law & Policy Review* 1 (1983), p. 270.

37. D. Nelson, "Carter's merit plan: a good first step," *Judicature* 61 (1977), p. 106.

38. Berkson and Carbon, *The United States Circuit Judge Nominating Commission,* pp. 97-99.

39. See U.S. Congress, Senate, *Selection and Confirmation of Federal Judges: Hearings before the Committee on the Judiciary,* 96th Cong., 1st sess., 1980, pp. 180, 534.

40. Telephone interview with Judge Griffin Bell, December 11, 1986.

41. Based on telephone interviews with Judge Bell (December 11, 1986), Michael Egan (December 8, 1986), Philip Modlin (December 9, 1986), and Drew Days (December 8, 1986). See also Judge Bell's testimony in U.S. Congress, Senate, *Nomination of Sherman E. Unger: Hearings before the Committee on the Judiciary,* 98th Cong., 1st sess., pt. 1, 1984, pp. 777-81. See also, G. Bell and R. Ostrow, *Taking Care of the Law* (New York: William Morrow & Co., 1982), pp. 39-42.

42. Quoted in R. Friedman and S. Wermiel, "Reagan Appointments to the Federal Bench Worry U.S. Liberals," *The Wall Street Journal,* September 6, 1985, p. A1.

43. R. Reagan, Message to the National Convention of the Knights of Columbus, August 5, 1986.

44. See H. Schwartz, *The New Right's Court Packing Campaign* (Washington, D.C.: People for the American Way, 1985); D. M. O'Brien, "Meese's Agenda for Ensuring the Reagan Legacy," *Los Angeles Times,* September 28, 1986, p. 3.

45. Markman, "A Comparison of Judicial Selection Procedures," p. 34.

46. Telephone interview with Bruce Fein, December 10, 1986. See also Office of Legal Policy, "Myths and Reality—Reagan Administration Judicial Selection," October 31, 1986, unpublished memorandum obtained from Deputy Assistant Attorney General Steve Matthews.

47. See U.S. Department of Justice, "Judicial selection procedures" (March 1981), reprinted in *Judicature* 64 (1981), p. 428. See also G. Fowler, "A Comparison of Initial Recommendation Procedures: Judicial Selection Under Reagan and Carter," *Yale Law & Policy Review* 1 (1983), p. 270.

48. Interviews with Philip A. Lacovara (October 28, 1986), John Lane (December 3, 1986), and several former members of the ABA Committee on

the Federal Judiciary. See also, P. Lacovara, "The Wrong Way to Pick Judges," *The New York Times,* October 3, 1986, p. A35.

49. Statement at panel on Reagan's Judges, Conference of Alliance for Justice, Washington, D.C., February 12, 1987.

50. S. Goldman, "Reaganizing the judiciary: the first term appointments," *Judicature* 68 (1985), p. 315.

51. National Public Radio, "All Things Considered," August 28, 1985.

52. Quoted in "Conservatives Pressing to Reshape Judiciary," *Congressional Quarterly Weekly Report,* September 7, 1985, p. 1759. E. Meese, address before the Palm Beach County Bar Association, February 10, 1986; and interviews with Department of Justice officials Terry Eastland (September 26, 1986), Dwight Rabuse (October 28, 1986), and Steve Matthews (October 28, 1986).

53. "All Things Considered," August 28, 1985 and October 2, 1984; excerpts quoted in U.S. Congress, Senate, *Confirmation Hearings on Federal Appointments: Hearings before the Committee on the Judiciary,* 95th Cong., 1st sess., pt. 2, pp. 430-31.

54. Quoted in "Justice Under Reagan," *U.S. News & World Report,* October 14, 1985, p. 65.

55. Interview with Philip A. Lacovara, October 28, 1986.

56. "All Things Considered," August 28, 1985.

57. Meese, address before the Palm Beach County Bar Association, February 10, 1986, p. 6.

58. Based on an interview with Reggie Govan, aide to Senator Joseph Biden, February 11, 1987; H. Kurtz, "GOP Senators Foiled on Judicial Nominees," *The Washington Post,* February 20, 1987; and S. Barr, "Judicial Tradeoff," *The Washington Post,* June 9, 1987.

59. See, e.g., "Judicial Committee Rejects Reagan Nominee," *Congressional Quarterly Weekly Report,* June 7, 1986, p. 1,297.

60. See U.S. Congress, Senate, *Nomination of Sherman E. Unger: Hearings before the Committee on the Judiciary,* 98th Cong., 1st sess., 1983.

61. See, e.g., U.S. Congress, Senate, *Confirmation Hearings on Federal Appointments: Hearings before the Committee on the Judiciary,* 99th Cong., 1st sess., 1985, p. 1,159, for Fitzwater; pp. 74-150 and 736-996 for Kozinski; and pp. 658-700 for Buckley; and compare floor debates.

62. See P. Shenon, "Opposed by Bar, Professor Fades as Judicial Choice," *The New York Times,* August 7, 1986, p. A1; and P. Traub, "Officials Deny I.U. Prof Picked for U.S. Court," *The Indianapolis Star,* June 28, 1986, p. 18.

63. Some "New Right" conservatives are already complaining about the rulings of some Reagan judges. See "Reagan's Court Revolution Comes Up Short," *U.S. News & World Report,* February 2, 1987, p. 2.

64. See Goldman, "Reaganizing the judiciary"; and S. Goldman, "Reagan's judicial appointments at mid-term: shaping the bench in his own image," *Judicature* 66 (1983), p. 335.

Chapter 4

1. P. Kurland, "Our Troubled Courts," *Nation's Business*, May 1971, p. 79.
2. Quoted by M. Freedman, *Assembly-Line Approval: A Common Cause Study of Senate Confirmation of Federal Judges* (Washington, D.C.: Common Cause, January 1986), p. 2.
3. See, e.g., O. Hatch, *Reagan and the Courts* (Washington, D.C.: Washington Legal Foundation, 1980); and P. Leahy, Statement to the Symposium on New Challenges in the Judicial Selection Process, Georgetown University Law Center, February 12, 1987.
4. Freedman, *Assembly-Line Approval*, p. 3.
5. Quoted by Senator Alan Cranston, in "The United States Senate's Responsibility In Judicial Confirmation Proceedings," *Congressional Record*, July 21, 1986, p. S9,342.
6. Ibid.
7. Letter from P. Kurland and L. Tribe to Senate Judiciary Committee, June 1, 1986. (Obtained from the Senate Judiciary Committee.)
8. See H. J. Abraham, *Justices and Presidents*, 2nd ed. (New York: Oxford University Press, 1985); and L. Tribe, *God Save This Honorable Court: How the Choice of Supreme Court Justices Shapes Our History* (New York: Random House, 1985).
9. J. Grossman, *Lawyers and Judges: The ABA and the Politics of Judicial Selection* (New York: John Wiley & Sons, 1965), p. 170.
10. See *Congressional Record,* November 6, 1985, pp. S14,926-S14,947.
11. Quoted in Judicial Selection Project, "Year End Report" (Washington, D.C.: Alliance for Justice, October 1986).
12. Quoted by J. Goulden, *The Benchwarmers* (New York: Random House, 1974), p. 34.
13. Quoted in "Here Come the Judges," *Time,* December 11, 1978, p. 112.
14. See Memorandum on Senatorial Courtesy, January 22, 1979, reprinted in U.S. Congress, Senate, *Selection and Confirmation of Federal Judges: Hearings Before the Committee on the Judiciary,* 96th Cong., 1st sess., 1980, pp. 118-22.
15. Quoted by N. Totenberg, "Will judges be chosen rationally?" *Judicature* 60 (1976), p. 94.
16. See U.S. Congress, Senate, *Confirmation of Federal Judges: Hearings before the Senate Judiciary Committee,* 97th Cong., 2d sess., 1982, p. 157.
17. See U.S. Congress, Senate, *Confirmation Hearings on Federal Appointments: Hearings before the Committee on the Judiciary,* 99th Cong., 1st sess., 1982, pt. 2, p. 1,163.
18. E. Slotnick, "Reforms in judicial selection: will they affect the Senate's role," *Judicature* 64 (1980), in two parts, starting at pp. 60 and 115.
19. R. Burke, "The Path to the Court: A Study of Federal Judicial Appointments" (unpublished dissertation, Vanderbilt University, Nashville, Tenn., 1958), p. 27.

20. Quoted by Goulden, *The Benchwarmers*, p. 27.

21. See Senator Kennedy's opening statement in *Selection and Confirmation of Federal Judges*, p. 1. Also, letter from Sheldon Goldman to Ken Feinberg, aide to Senator Kennedy, September 7, 1978. (The author expresses his appreciation to Professor Goldman for making this letter available.)

22. See "Kennedy and Rodino: How Two Very Different Chairmen Run Their Panels," *Congressional Quarterly Weekly Report*, February 2, 1980, p. 267; and E. Slotnick, "The changing role of the Senate Judiciary Committee in judicial selection," *Judicature* 62 (1979), p. 502.

23. Based on telephone interviews with Thomas Sussman (December 8, 1986) and Elaine Shocas (December 9, 1986).

24. Interview with Elaine Jones (October 28, 1986).

25. Interview with Senate staff member (not for attribution).

26. Quoted in *Report of the National Bar Association on Jefferson Beauregard Sessions, III, for Appointment to the Federal District Court for the Southern District of Alabama* (copy made available to the author by Elaine Jones).

27. See H. Kurtz, "Reagan Pick for Judgeship Is Rejected," *The Washington Post*, March 21, 1986, p. A1; and "Sessions Called Unfit," *Congressional Quarterly Weekly Report*, June 7, 1986, p. 1,297.

28. Quoted by H. Kurtz, "Democrats Try to Slow Confirmation of Judges," *The Washington Post*, November 12, 1985, p. A3.

29. Interviews with Reggie Govan (December 5, 1986) and Laurie Westley, aide to Senator Simon (December 3, 1986).

30. Quoted by H. Kurtz, "Reagan Pick For Judgeship Is Rejected," and interview with Nan Aron and Nancy Broff (October 29, 1986).

31. P. Leahy, Statement to the Symposium on New Challenges in the Judicial Selection Process, February 8, 1987, Washington, D.C.

32. Ibid.

33. For discussion of the Senate's rejections of nominees to the Supreme Court, see C. Warren, *The Supreme Court in the United States History*, 1st ed. (Boston: Little, Brown, 1922); W. Swindler, "The Politics of 'Advice and Consent,'" *American Bar Association Journal* 56 (1970), p. 533; Abraham, *Justices and Presidents;* and Tribe, *God Save This Honorable Court.*

34. See J. Thorpe, "The Appearance of Supreme Court Nominees Before the Senate Judiciary Committee," *Journal of Public Law* 18 (1969), p. 371.

35. For a more elaborate articulation of this view, see former assistant attorney general in the Reagan administration Grover Rees's article, "Questions for Supreme Court Nominees at Confirmation Hearings: Excluding the Constitution," *Georgia Law Review* 17 (1983), p. 913.

36. Quoted by A. Cranston, "The United States Senate's Responsibility in Judicial Confirmation Proceedings," *Congressional Record*, July 21, 1986, p. S9,341.

37. F. Frankfurter, "The Supreme Court and the Public," *Forum* 83 (1930), p. 334.

38. See U.S. Congress, Senate, *Hearings Before the Senate Judiciary Committee on Nominations of Abe Fortas and Homer Thornberry,* 90th Cong., 2d sess., 1968, p. 180.

39. See *Congressional Record,* p. 24655 and U.S. Congress, Senate, *Hearings Before the Senate Judiciary on the Nomination of Thurgood Marshall,* 90th Cong., 1st sess., 1967, p. 387.

40. See U.S. Congress, Senate, *Senate Executive Report No. 92-16,* 92d Cong., 1st sess., 1971, pp. 27, 55.

41. Statements at confirmation hearings on Chief Justice William Rehnquist from unpublished transcript obtained from the Senate Judiciary Committee.

42. L. Paper, Memorandum to Senator Joseph Biden, *Senate's Advice and Consent to Supreme Court Nomination,* July 18, 1986. (Obtained from the Senate Judiciary Committee.)

43. D. Lively, "The Supreme Court Appointment Process: In Search of Constitutional Roles and Responsibilities," *Southern California Law Review* 59 (1986), p. 563.

44. W. Rehnquist, "The Making of a Supreme Court Justice," *Harvard Law Record* 29 (1959), p. 7.

45. Letter to Senator Fannin and quoted in *Congressional Record* 114, p. 28,756.

46. See, e.g., Paper, Memorandum to Senator Biden, July 18, 1986; Leahy, Statement to the Symposium on New Challenges in the Judicial Selection Process; P. Simon, "The Senate's Role in Judicial Appointments," speech before the National Press Club, Washington, D.C., March 10, 1986; and R. Friedman, "The Transformation in Senate Response to Supreme Court Nominations: From Reconstruction to the Taft Administration and Beyond," *Cardozo Law Review* 5 (1984), p. 1.

47. Tribe, *God Save This Honorable Court.*

48. Based on Freedman, *Assembly-Line Approval;* and interviews with Jones (October 28, 1986), Aron and Broff (October 29, 1986), and Melanne Verveer, director of public policy for People for the American Way (October 29, 1986).

Chapter 5

1. See American Bar Association, *The ABA's Standing Committee on Federal Judiciary: What It Is and How It Works* (Chicago: American Bar Association, 1983); and H. Chase, *Federal Judges: The Appointing Process* (Minneapolis: University of Minnesota Press, 1972).

2. See J. Schmidhauser, *Judges and Justices: The Federal Appellate Judiciary* (Boston: Little, Brown, 1979), pp. 23-26.

3. See J. Grossman, *Lawyers and Judges: The ABA and the Politics of Judicial Selection* (New York: Wiley, 1965).

4. P. Reidinger, "Rating the Reagan Judges," *American Bar Association Journal* 73, April 1, 1987, p. 44.

5. P. Kurland, "The Appointment and Disappointment of Supreme Court Justices," *Law and Social Order* (1972), p. 212.

6. Quotations from "WLF Loses ABA Suit," *American Bar Association Journal* 73, March 1, 1987, p. 19; briefs in *Washington Legal Foundation v. American Bar Association Standing Committee on Federal Judiciary*, Civil Action 85-3918, U.S. District Court for the District of Columbia, November 6, 1986 (obtained from the ABA and the Washington Legal Foundation); P. Kamenar, "Behind Closed Doors: How the ABA Vetos Judicial Nominations," *Benchmark* 2 (1985), p. 11; and interview with Paul Kamenar (October 28, 1986).

7. *Washington Legal Foundation v. American Bar Association Standing Committee on Federal Judiciary*, Civil Action 85-3918, November 26, 1986.

8. See American Bar Association, *The ABA's Standing Committee on Federal Judiciary*, p. 7; and compare, *Defendant's Memorandum of Points and Authorities in Support of Motion to Dismiss, Washington Legal Foundation v. American Bar Association Standing Committee on Federal Judiciary*, Civil Action 85-3918, pp. 7-8 and 40. Also see statements of Robert Raven, former chairman of the ABA Committee on Federal Judiciary, in "The federal judiciary: what role politics?" *Judicature* 68 (1985), p. 330.

9. Letter from Robert Fiske, chairman of ABA Standing Committee on Federal Judiciary to Paul Kamenar, November 27, 1985; and interview with Kamenar (October 28, 1986).

10. Interviews with John Lane (December 3, 1986) and others from the ABA and the Justice Department (who wanted their statements to be off the record). Thomas's statements are quoted by A. Kamen, "Under Conservative Pressure, ABA Drops Judicial Panelist," *The Washington Post,* July 18, 1986, p. A2.

11. Statement of Senator Simon during the confirmation hearings on Chief Justice William Rehnquist (from an unpublished transcript made available by the staff of the Senate Judiciary Committee).

12. American Bar Association, *Opinions of the Committee on Professional Ethics and Grievances* (Chicago: American Bar Association, 1957), p. 226; quoted by Grossman, *Lawyers and Judges,* p. 50.

13. Quoted by A. T. Mason, *Brandeis: A Free Man's Life* (New York: Viking, 1946), p. 489.

14. Grossman, *Lawyers and Judges,* p. 52. See also Schmidhauser, *Judges and Justices,* p. 230.

15. See, e.g., W. Armstrong, "The Increasing Importance of State Supreme Courts," *American Bar Association Journal* 28 (1942), p. 3; J. Douglas, "Judicial Selection and Tenure: Missouri Plan," *American Bar Association Journal* 33 (1947), p. 1,169; M. Smith, "The California Method of Selecting Judges," *Stanford Law Review* 3 (1951), p. 571. For a good survey of state judicial selection methods, see L. Berkson, S. Beller, and M. Grimaldi, *Judicial Selection in the United States: A Compendium of Provisions* (Chicago: American Judicature Society, 1981); and L. Berkson, "Judicial selection in the United States: a special report," *Judicature* 64 (1980), p. 176.

16. See "Appointments to the Bench: Association Seeks High Standards of Qualifications," *American Bar Association Journal* 32 (1946), p. 823 (emphasis added); and Editorial, "Thoughts on Federal Judicial Appointments," *Journal of the American Judicature Society* 29 (1945), p. 100.

17. See J. Buchanan, "Choosing Federal Judges: The Continuing Struggle for Good Judges," *American Bar Association Journal* 33 (1947), p. 537.

18. See B. Miller, "Federal Judicial Appointments: The Continuing Struggle for Good Judges," *American Bar Association Journal* 41 (1955), p. 127.

19. Quoted in testimony of Bernard Segal, U.S. Congress, Senate, *Judicial Fitness: Hearings before the Subcommittee on Improvements in Judicial Machinery*, 89th Cong., 2d sess., 1966, pt. 1, p. 46. See also B. Segal, "Federal Judicial Selection—Progress and the Promise of the Future," *Massachusetts Law Quarterly* (1961), p. 138.

20. Segal, *Judicial Fitness*, p. 48.

21. Quoted by Grossman, *Lawyers and Judges*, p. 79.

22. See "Meskill Judgeship Approved After Long Delay," *Congressional Quarterly Weekly Report*, April 26, 1975, p. 893, and September 21, 1974, pp. 2,570- 2,571.

23. See U.S. Congress, Senate, *Selection and Confirmation of Federal Judges: Hearings before the Committee on the Judiciary*, 99th Cong., 1st and 2d sess., 1980, pt. 6.

24. See U.S. Congress, Senate, *Nomination of Sherman E. Unger: Hearing before the Committee on the Judiciary*, 98th Cong., 1st sess., 1983 (three parts).

25. Alliance for Justice Newsletter, January 1987, p. 1.

26. While a number of officials in the Reagan administration deny looking for younger judges, Fred Fielding has admitted that that was its policy in judicial recruitment. Interview with Nina Totenberg, "All Things Considered," National Public Radio, October 2, 1984.

27. Chase, *Federal Judges*, p. 179; data on the Carter and Reagan appointees is based on materials provided by the Department of Justice and the American Bar Association.

28. See S. Taylor, "Reagan Puts Ideology First in Filling Vacancies," *The New York Times*, April 22, 1984, p. E5; P. Smith, "Wilkinson Judgeship Lobby Was Extensive, Senate Panel Hears," *The Washington Post*, August 8, 1984, p. D1; and U.S. Congress, Senate, *Confirmation Hearings on Federal Appointments: Hearings before the Committee on the Judiciary*, 98th Cong., 2d sess., 1984, pt. 3.

29. Based on conversations with Elaine Jones of the NAACP Legal Defense Fund (October 28, 1986, and February 25, 1987).

30. See Healy, "Carter Won't Name Cox to Federal Judgeship," *Boston Globe*, August 3, 1979, p. A1.

31. For a good discussion of this issue with Brooksley Born, see E. Slotnick, "The ABA Standing Committee on Federal Judiciary: a contemporary assessment," *Judicature* 67 (1983), pt. 1, pp. 356-57.

32. Interview with Philip Lacovara (October 28, 1986).

33. Telephone interview with Edward Levi (December 19, 1986).

34. Quoted by Slotnick, "The ABA Standing Committee on Federal Judiciary," pt. 1, p. 361.

35. Grossman, *Lawyers and Judges,* pp. 76-77.

36. See J. Goulden, *The Benchwarmers* (New York: Random House, 1974), p. 56.

37. Chase, *Federal Judges,* p. 135.

38. Quoted by Slotnick, "The ABA Standing Committee on Federal Judiciary," pt. 1, p. 360.

39. See ibid. and telephone interview with Born (December 19, 1986).

40. Telephone interview with Griffin Bell (December 11, 1986).

41. Quoted by Slotnick, "The ABA Standing Committee on Federal Judiciary," p. 353.

42. Telephone interview with Bruce Fein (December 10, 1986).

43. Quoted by P. Schuck, *The Judiciary Committee* (New York: Grossman, 1975), p. 230.

44. Based on data in a letter from former chairman of the ABA Committee on Federal Judiciary, Frederick Buesser, Jr., to Senator Strom Thurmond; reprinted in U.S. Congress, Senate, *Selection and Confirmation of Federal Judges: Hearings before the Committee on the Judiciary,* 96th Cong., 1st sess., 1979, pp. 318-24.

45. Schuck, *The Judiciary Committee,* p. 240.

Chapter 6

1. See H. Kurtz, "For Reagan, Clock Ticking on Judgeships," *The Washington Post,* May 22, 1987, p. A23; and S. Goldman, "Reagan's second term judicial appointments: the battle at midway," *Judicature* 70 (1987), p. 324.

2. M. Cuomo, "Keynote Address," American Bar Association, August 11, 1986, pp. 16-17 (supplied by the governor's office).

3. See J. Stennis, "Federal Judiciary Selection: The Letter—But the Spirit?" *American Bar Association Journal* 44 (1958), p. 1,179; and C. Bloch, "The Selection of Federal Judges," *American Bar Association Journal* 41 (1955), p. 510.

4. See Memorandum to the President, "The Appointment of Federal Judges," April 15, 1958, Dwight David Eisenhower Diaries, Box 32, Eisenhower Presidential Library. For a discussion of the history of these early proposals, see J. Grossman, *Lawyers and Judges: The ABA and the Politics of Judicial Selection* (New York: John Wiley & Sons, 1965), p. 130.

5. See H. Scott, "The Selection of Federal Judges," *Washington and Lee Law Review* 24 (1967), p. 205.

6. See, e.g., G. Winters, "Merit Selection of Federal Judges," in G. Winters, ed., *Judicial Selection and Tenure: Selected Readings* (Chicago: American Judicature Society, 1973); and Editorial, *Judicature* 52 (1968), p. 93. Chief Judge

Helen Nies of the Court of Appeals for the Federal Circuit recently endorsed the idea of creating such a commission for judicial selection. See her testimony in U.S. Congress, Senate, *Nomination of Sherman E. Unger: Hearing before the Committee on the Judiciary,* 98th Cong., 1st sess., 1983, pt. 1, pp. 41-43.

7. For a perceptive critique of Senator Scott's proposal, see S. Goldman, "Political selection of federal judges and the proposal for a judicial service commission," *Judicature* 52 (1968), p. 94.

8. See, e.g., R. Watson and R. Downing, *The Politics of the Bench and the Bar* (New York: John Wiley & Sons, 1969).

Epilogue

1. For further discussion, see D. M. O'Brien, "Meese's Agenda for Ensuring the Reagan Legacy," *Los Angeles Times,* September 28, 1987, p. 1; D. M. O'Brien, "Reagan's Legacy for U.S. Courts," *Los Angeles Times,* August 20, 1987, p. 1; D. M. O'Brien, "Ginsburg and the Chicago School of Thought," *Los Angeles Times,* November 8, 1987, p. 1; and D. M. O'Brien, "Reagan Judges: His Most Enduring Legacy?" in C. O. Jones, ed., *Reagan's Legacy* (Chatham, N.J.: Chatham House, 1988).

2. See L. Greenhouse, "Reagan's Advisors See Shift in Focus as Influence at Capitol Drops Slightly," *The New York Times,* August 23, 1987, p. A23.

3. A. Kornhauser, "Liberal Groups Take Early Jump in Bork Battle," *Legal Times,* July 20, 1987, p. 6.

4. E. Walsh, "ACLU Urges Senate to Reject Bork's Nomination to the Court," *The Washington Post,* September 1, 1987, p. 44; E. Walsh, "AFL-CIO Asks Senate to Disapprove Bork," *The Washington Post,* August 18, 1987, p. A1.

5. The reports appear in *Cardozo Law Review* 9 (1987), pp. 187-218 and 373-508.

6. Quoted by S. Roberts, "Reagan Implores the Public to Aid in Fight for Bork," *The New York Times,* October 14, 1987, p. A1.

7. L. Greenhouse, "Bork as a Bonanza," *The New York Times,* September 11, 1987, p. A1.

8. Reagan speech to convention of Concerned Women for America, quoted by B. McAllister and C. Robertson, "Critics Fail to Realize Bork Is in Judicial 'Mainstream,' Reagan Charges," *The Washington Post,* September 26, 1987, p. A6.

9. K. Karpay, "The Selling of Bork: In *Legal Times* Interview, Judge Touts Open-Mindedness," *Legal Times,* July 20, 1987, p. 1.

10. Quoted by R. Collins and D. M. O'Brien, "Just Where Does Judge Bork Stand?" *The National Law Journal,* September 7, 1987, p. 13.

11. Quoted in "Working the Bork Hearings," *Legal Times,* September 21, 1987, p. 1.

12. See S. Taylor, "In Un-Socratic Exchanges, Bork Delineates Several Selves," *The New York Times,* September 30, 1987, p. A1; and A. Kamen, "Bork v. Bork," *The Washington Post,* September 23, 1987, p. A19.

13. Quoted by S. Taylor, "How Bork Recast Ideas in His Senate Testimony," *The New York Times*, September 21, 1987, p. B14; and Kamen, "Bork v. Bork."

14. Quoted and discussed by D. M. O'Brien and R. Collins, "Bork's Shifts Made Credibility an Issue," *The Baltimore Sun*, October 11, 1987, p. K1.

15. Taylor, "How Bork Recast Ideas in His Senate Testimony."

16. T. Moran, "Scenes from the Bork Hearings," *Legal Times*, September 21, 1987, p. 7.

17. S. Taylor, "Justice Stevens, in Unusual Move, Praises Bork as Nominee to Court," *The New York Times*, August 1, 1987, p. A1; A. Kamen, "How White 'Endorsed' Judge Bork," *The Washington Post*, September 23, 1987, p. A19.

18. See E. Meese, "The Attorney General's View of the Supreme Court: Toward a Return to a Jurisprudence on Original Intention," in C. Wise and D. M. O'Brien, eds., *Law and Public Affairs*, (special issue of) *Public Administration Review* 45 (1985). See also L. Greenhouse, "The Bork Battle: Visions of the Constitution," *The New York Times*, October 4, 1987, sec. 4, p. 1.

19. See N. Cohodas, "Senate Warms Up for 'Divisive' Bork Debate," *Congressional Quarterly Weekly Report*, October 17, 1987, p. 2512.

20. See "Gone with the Wind: Southern Senators May Doom the Bork Nomination," *Time*, October 12, 1987, p. 18.

21. Quoted by J. Brinkley, "Reagan Intensifies Campaign to Win Bork Nomination," *The New York Times*, October 1, 1987, p. A1. Bork statement after vote of Senate Judiciary Committee, appearing in *Congressional Quarterly Weekly Report*, October 10, 1987, p. 2435.

22. Quoted by L. Greenhouse, "A Vote against Bork and against Reagan's Agenda," *International Herald Tribune*, October 8, 1987, p. 1.

23. See E. Walsh, "Bork Panel Likely to Take Neutral Stand," *The Washington Post*, September 30, 1987, p. A4; and D. Russakoff, "In Dixie, Black Vote and Savvy Senator Hurt Bork," *International Herald Tribune*, October 9, 1987, p. 5.

24. For a further discussion, see O'Brien, "Ginsburg and the Chicago School of Thought."

25. See N. Cohodas, "Ginsburg Hurt Badly by Marijuana Admission," *Congressional Quarterly Weekly Report*, November 7, 1987, p. 2714.

Index